HBR's 10 Must Reads

UPDATED &
EXPANDED

High
Performance

HBR's 10 Must Reads

HBR's 10 Must Reads are definitive collections of classic ideas, practical advice, and essential thinking from the pages of *Harvard Business Review*. Exploring topics like disruptive innovation, emotional intelligence, and new technology in our ever-evolving world, these books empower any leader to make bold decisions and inspire others.

TITLES INCLUDE:

HBR's 10 Must Reads for New Managers
HBR's 10 Must Reads on AI
HBR's 10 Must Reads on Building a Great Culture
HBR's 10 Must Reads on Change Management
HBR's 10 Must Reads on Communication
HBR's 10 Must Reads on Data Strategy
HBR's 10 Must Reads on Decision-Making
HBR's 10 Must Reads on Design Thinking
HBR's 10 Must Reads on Digital Transformation
HBR's 10 Must Reads on Emotional Intelligence
HBR's 10 Must Reads on High Performance
HBR's 10 Must Reads on Innovation
HBR's 10 Must Reads on Leadership
HBR's 10 Must Reads on Leading Winning Teams
HBR's 10 Must Reads on Managing People
HBR's 10 Must Reads on Managing Yourself
HBR's 10 Must Reads on Marketing
HBR's 10 Must Reads on Mental Toughness
HBR's 10 Must Reads on Strategy
HBR's 10 Must Reads on Women and Leadership
HBR's 10 Must Reads Boxed Set (6 Books)
HBR's 10 Must Reads Ultimate Boxed Set (14 Books)

For a full list, visit hbr.org/mustreads.

HBR's 10 Must Reads

UPDATED & EXPANDED

High Performance

Harvard Business Review Press
Boston, Massachusetts

Copyright 2025 Harvard Business School Publishing Corporation

All rights reserved

Printed in the United States of America

10 9 8 7 6 5 4 3 2 1

No part of this publication may be reproduced, stored in or introduced into a retrieval system, or transmitted, in any form, or by any means (electronic, mechanical, photocopying, recording, or otherwise), without the prior permission of the publisher. Requests for permission should be directed to permissions@harvardbusiness.org, or mailed to Permissions, Harvard Business School Publishing, 60 Harvard Way, Boston, Massachusetts 02163.

The web addresses referenced in this book were live and correct at the time of the book's publication but may be subject to change.

Library of Congress Cataloging-in-Publication Data

Names: Harvard Business Review Press issuing body
Title: HBR's 10 must reads. High performance
Other titles: HBR's 10 must reads on high performance. | High performance
Description: Updated and expanded [edition]. | Boston, Massachusetts : Harvard Business Review Press, [2025] | Series: HBR's 10 must reads | Earlier edition published in 2022 as: HBR's 10 must reads on high performance.
Identifiers: LCCN 2025001513 (print) | LCCN 2025001514 (ebook) | ISBN 9798892791793 paperback alk. paper | ISBN 9798892791809 epub
Subjects: LCSH: Work—Psychological aspects | Performance | Success in business
Classification: LCC BF481 .H397 2025 (print) | LCC BF481 (ebook) | DDC 158.7—dc23/eng/20250501
LC record available at https://lccn.loc.gov/2025001513
LC ebook record available at https://lccn.loc.gov/2025001514

ISBN: 979-8-89279-179-3
eISBN: 979-8-89279-180-9

The paper used in this publication meets the requirements of the American National Standard for Permanence of Paper for Publications and Documents in Libraries and Archives Z39.48-1992.

Contents

UPDATED &
EXPANDED

High
Performance

1

The Focused Leader

by Daniel Goleman

A primary task of leadership is to direct attention. To do so, leaders must learn to focus their own attention. When we speak about being focused, we commonly mean thinking about one thing while filtering out distractions. But a wealth of recent research in neuroscience shows that we focus in many ways, for different purposes, drawing on different neural pathways—some of which work in concert, while others tend to stand in opposition.

Grouping these modes of attention into three broad buckets—focusing on *yourself*, focusing on *others*, and focusing on *the wider world*—sheds new light on the practice of many essential leadership skills. Focusing inward and focusing constructively on others helps leaders cultivate the primary elements of emotional intelligence. A fuller understanding of how they focus on the wider world can improve their ability to devise strategy, innovate, and manage organizations.

Every leader needs to cultivate this triad of awareness, in abundance and in the proper balance, because a failure to focus inward leaves you rudderless, a failure to focus on others renders you clueless, and a failure to focus outward may leave you blindsided.

Focusing on Yourself

Emotional intelligence begins with self-awareness—getting in touch with your inner voice. Leaders who heed their inner voices can draw on more resources to make better decisions and connect with their authentic selves. But what does that entail? A look at how people focus inward can make this abstract concept more concrete.

Self-awareness

Hearing your inner voice is a matter of paying careful attention to internal physiological signals. These subtle cues are monitored by the insula, which is tucked behind the frontal lobes of the brain. Attention given to any part of the body amps up the insula's sensitivity to that part. Tune in to your heartbeat, and the insula activates more neurons in that circuitry. How well people can sense their heartbeats has, in fact, become a standard way to measure their self-awareness.

Gut feelings are messages from the insula and the amygdala, which the neuroscientist Antonio Damasio, of the University of Southern California, calls *somatic markers*. Those messages are sensations that something "feels" right or wrong. Somatic markers simplify decision-making by guiding our attention toward better options. They're hardly foolproof (how often was that feeling that you left the stove on correct?), so the more comprehensively we read them, the better we use our intuition. (See the sidebar "Are You Skimming This Sidebar?")

Idea in Brief

The Problem

A primary task of leadership is to direct attention. To do so, leaders must learn to focus their own attention.

The Argument

People commonly think of "being focused" as filtering out distractions while concentrating on one thing. But a wealth of recent neuroscience research shows that we focus attention in many ways, for different purposes, while drawing on different neural pathways.

The Solution

Every leader needs to cultivate a triad of awareness—an inward focus, a focus on others, and an outward focus. Focusing inward and focusing on others helps leaders cultivate emotional intelligence. Focusing outward can improve their ability to devise strategy, innovate, and manage organizations.

Consider, for example, the implications of an analysis of interviews conducted by a group of British researchers with 118 professional traders and 10 senior managers at four City of London investment banks. The most successful traders (whose annual income averaged £500,000) were neither the ones who relied entirely on analytics nor the ones who just went with their guts. They focused on a full range of emotions, which they used to judge the value of their intuition. When they suffered losses, they acknowledged their anxiety, became more cautious, and took fewer risks. The least successful traders (whose income averaged only £100,000) tended to ignore their anxiety and keep going with their guts. Because they failed to heed a wider array of internal signals, they were misled.

Zeroing in on sensory impressions of ourselves in the moment is one major element of self-awareness. But another is critical to

Are You Skimming This Sidebar?

Do you have trouble remembering what someone has just told you in conversation? Did you drive to work this morning on autopilot? Do you focus more on your smartphone than on the person you're having lunch with?

Attention is a mental muscle; like any other muscle, it can be strengthened through the right kind of exercise. The fundamental rep for building deliberate attention is simple: When your mind wanders, notice that it has wandered, bring it back to your desired point of focus, and keep it there as long as you can. That basic exercise is at the root of virtually every kind of meditation. Meditation builds concentration and calmness and facilitates recovery from the agitation of stress.

So does a video game called Tenacity, now in development by a design group and neuroscientists at the University of Wisconsin. Slated for release in 2014, the game offers a leisurely journey through any of half a dozen scenes, from a barren desert to a fantasy staircase spiraling heavenward. At the beginner's level you tap an iPad screen with one finger every time you exhale; the challenge is to tap two fingers with every fifth breath. As you move to higher levels, you're presented with more distractions—a helicopter flies into view, a plane does a flip, a flock of birds suddenly scud by.

When players are attuned to the rhythm of their breathing, they experience the strengthening of selective attention as a feeling of calm focus, as in meditation. Stanford University is exploring that connection at its Calming Technology Lab, which is developing relaxing devices, such as a belt that detects your breathing rate. Should a chock-full in-box, for instance, trigger what has been called email apnea, an iPhone app can guide you through exercises to calm your breathing and your mind.

leadership: combining our experiences across time into a coherent view of our authentic selves.

To be authentic is to be the same person to others as you are to yourself. In part that entails paying attention to what others think of you, particularly people whose opinions you esteem and

Expand Your Awareness

Just as a camera lens can be set narrowly on a single point or more widely to take in a panoramic view, you can focus tightly or expansively.

One measure of open awareness presents people with a stream of letters and numbers, such as S, K, O, E, 4, R, T, 2, H, P. In scanning the stream, many people will notice the first number, 4, but after that their attention blinks. Those firmly in open awareness mode will register the second number as well.

Strengthening the ability to maintain open awareness requires leaders to do something that verges on the unnatural: cultivate at least sometimes a willingness to not be in control, not offer up their own views, not judge others. That's less a matter of deliberate action than of attitude adjustment.

One path to making that adjustment is through the classic power of positive thinking, because pessimism narrows our focus, whereas positive emotions widen our attention and our receptiveness to the new and unexpected. A simple way to shift into positive mode is to ask yourself, "If everything worked out perfectly in my life, what would I be doing in 10 years?" Why is that effective? Because when you're in an upbeat mood, the University of Wisconsin neuroscientist Richard Davidson has found, your brain's left prefrontal area lights up. That area harbors the circuitry that reminds us how great we'll feel when we reach some long-sought goal.

"Talking about positive goals and dreams activates brain centers that open you up to new possibilities," says Richard Boyatzis, a psychologist at Case Western Reserve. "But if you change the conversation to what you should do to fix yourself, it closes you down. . . . You need the negative to survive, but the positive to thrive."

who will be candid in their feedback. A variety of focus that is useful here is *open awareness*, in which we broadly notice what's going on around us without getting caught up in or swept away by any particular thing. In this mode we don't judge, censor, or tune out; we simply perceive.

Leaders who are more accustomed to giving input than to receiving it may find this tricky. Someone who has trouble sustaining open awareness typically gets snagged by irritating details, such as fellow travelers in the airport security line who take forever getting their carry-ons into the scanner. Someone who can keep her attention in open mode will notice the travelers but not worry about them, and will take in more of her surroundings. (See the sidebar "Expand Your Awareness.")

Of course, being open to input doesn't guarantee that someone will provide it. Sadly, life affords us few chances to learn how others really see us, and even fewer for executives as they rise through the ranks. That may be why one of the most popular and overenrolled courses at Harvard Business School is Bill George's Authentic Leadership Development, in which George has created what he calls True North groups to heighten this aspect of self-awareness.

These groups (which anyone can form) are based on the precept that self-knowledge begins with self-revelation. Accordingly, they are open and intimate, "a safe place," George explains, "where members can discuss personal issues they do not feel they can raise elsewhere—often not even with their closest family members." What good does that do? "We don't know who we are until we hear ourselves speaking the story of our lives to those we trust," George says. It's a structured way to match our view of our true selves with the views our most trusted colleagues have—an external check on our authenticity.

Self-control

"Cognitive control" is the scientific term for putting one's attention where one wants it and keeping it there in the face of temptation to wander. This focus is one aspect of the brain's executive function, which is located in the prefrontal cortex. A colloquial term for it is "willpower."

Cognitive control enables executives to pursue a goal despite distractions and setbacks. The same neural circuitry that allows such a single-minded pursuit of goals also manages unruly emotions. Good cognitive control can be seen in people who stay calm in a crisis, tame their own agitation, and recover from a debacle or defeat.

Decades' worth of research demonstrates the singular importance of willpower to leadership success. Particularly compelling is a longitudinal study tracking the fates of all 1,037 children born during a single year in the 1970s in the New Zealand city of Dunedin. For several years during childhood the children were given a battery of tests of willpower, including the psychologist Walter Mischel's legendary "marshmallow test"—a choice between eating one marshmallow right away and getting two by waiting 15 minutes. In Mischel's experiments, roughly a third of children grab the marshmallow on the spot, another third hold out for a while longer, and a third manage to make it through the entire quarter hour.

Years later, when the children in the Dunedin study were in their 30s and all but 4% of them had been tracked down again, the researchers found that those who'd had the cognitive control to resist the marshmallow longest were significantly healthier, more successful financially, and more law-abiding than the ones who'd been unable to hold out at all. In fact, statistical analysis showed that a child's level of self-control was a more powerful predictor of financial success than IQ, social class, or family circumstance.

How we focus holds the key to exercising willpower, Mischel says. Three subvarieties of cognitive control are at play when you pit self-restraint against self-gratification: the ability to voluntarily disengage your focus from an object of desire; the ability to

Learning Self-Restraint

Quick, now. Here's a test of cognitive control. In what direction is the middle arrow in each row pointing?

The test, called the Eriksen Flanker Task, gauges your susceptibility to distraction. When it's taken under laboratory conditions, differences of a thousandth of a second can be detected in the speed with which subjects perceive which direction the middle arrows are pointing. The stronger their cognitive control, the less susceptible they are to distraction.

Interventions to strengthen cognitive control can be as unsophisticated as a game of Simon Says or Red Light—any exercise in which you are asked to stop on cue. Research suggests that the better a child gets at playing Musical Chairs, the stronger his or her prefrontal wiring for cognitive control will become.

Operating on a similarly simple principle is a social and emotional learning (SEL) method that's used to strengthen cognitive control in schoolchildren across the United States. When confronted by an upsetting problem, the children are told to think of a traffic signal. The red light means stop, calm down, and think before you act. The yellow light means slow down and think of several possible solutions. The green light means try out a plan and see how it works. Thinking in these terms allows the children to shift away from amygdala-driven impulses to prefrontal-driven deliberate behavior.

It's never too late for adults to strengthen these circuits as well. Daily sessions of mindfulness practice work in a way similar to Musical Chairs and SEL. In these sessions you focus your attention on your breathing and practice tracking your thoughts and feelings without getting swept away by them. Whenever you notice that your mind has wandered, you simply return it to your breath. It sounds easy—but try it for 10 minutes, and you'll find there's a learning curve.

resist distraction so that you don't gravitate back to that object; and the ability to concentrate on the future goal and imagine how good you will feel when you achieve it. As adults the children of Dunedin may have been held hostage to their younger selves, but they need not have been, because the power to focus can be developed. (See the sidebar "Learning Self-Restraint.")

Focusing on Others

The word "attention" comes from the Latin *attendere*, meaning "to reach toward." This is a perfect definition of focus on others, which is the foundation of empathy and of an ability to build social relationships—the second and third pillars of emotional intelligence.

Executives who can effectively focus on others are easy to recognize. They are the ones who find common ground, whose opinions carry the most weight, and with whom other people want to work. They emerge as natural leaders regardless of organizational or social rank.

The empathy triad

We talk about empathy most commonly as a single attribute. But a close look at where leaders are focusing when they exhibit it reveals three distinct kinds, each important for leadership effectiveness:

- *cognitive empathy*—the ability to understand another person's perspective;

- *emotional empathy*—the ability to feel what someone else feels;

- *empathic concern*—the ability to sense what another person needs from you.

Cognitive empathy enables leaders to explain themselves in meaningful ways—a skill essential to getting the best performance from their direct reports. Contrary to what you might expect, exercising cognitive empathy requires leaders to think about feelings rather than to feel them directly.

An inquisitive nature feeds cognitive empathy. As one successful executive with this trait puts it, "I've always just wanted to learn everything, to understand anybody that I was around— why they thought what they did, why they did what they did, what worked for them, and what didn't work." But cognitive empathy is also an outgrowth of self-awareness. The executive circuits that allow us to think about our own thoughts and to monitor the feelings that flow from them let us apply the same reasoning to other people's minds when we choose to direct our attention that way.

Emotional empathy is important for effective mentoring, managing clients, and reading group dynamics. It springs from ancient parts of the brain beneath the cortex—the amygdala, the hypothalamus, the hippocampus, and the orbitofrontal cortex— that allow us to feel fast without thinking deeply. They tune us in by arousing in our bodies the emotional states of others: I literally feel your pain. My brain patterns match up with yours when I listen to you tell a gripping story. As Tania Singer, the director of the social neuroscience department at the Max Planck Institute for Human Cognitive and Brain Sciences, in Leipzig, says, "You need to understand your own feelings to understand the feelings of others." Accessing your capacity for emotional empathy depends on combining two kinds of attention: a deliberate focus on your own echoes of someone else's feelings and an open awareness of that person's face, voice, and other external signs of emotion. (See the sidebar "When Empathy Needs to Be Learned.")

When Empathy Needs to Be Learned

Emotional empathy can be developed. That's the conclusion suggested by research conducted with physicians by Helen Riess, the director of the Empathy and Relational Science Program at Boston's Massachusetts General Hospital. To help the physicians monitor themselves, she set up a program in which they learned to focus using deep, diaphragmatic breathing and to cultivate a certain detachment—to watch an interaction from the ceiling, as it were, rather than being lost in their own thoughts and feelings. "Suspending your own involvement to observe what's going on gives you a mindful awareness of the interaction without being completely reactive," says Riess. "You can see if your own physiology is charged up or balanced. You can notice what's transpiring in the situation." If a doctor realizes that she's feeling irritated, for instance, that may be a signal that the patient is bothered too.

Those who are utterly at a loss may be able to prime emotional empathy essentially by faking it until they make it, Riess adds. If you act in a caring way—looking people in the eye and paying attention to their expressions, even when you don't particularly want to—you may start to feel more engaged.

Empathic concern, which is closely related to emotional empathy, enables you to sense not just how people feel but what they need from you. It's what you want in your doctor, your spouse—and your boss. Empathic concern has its roots in the circuitry that compels parents' attention to their children. Watch where people's eyes go when someone brings an adorable baby into a room, and you'll see this mammalian brain center leaping into action.

One neural theory holds that the response is triggered in the amygdala by the brain's radar for sensing danger and in the prefrontal cortex by the release of oxytocin, the chemical for caring. This implies that empathic concern is a double-edged feeling. We intuitively experience the distress of another as our own. But in deciding whether we will meet that person's needs, we deliberately weigh how much we value his or her well-being.

Getting this intuition-deliberation mix right has great implications. Those whose sympathetic feelings become too strong may themselves suffer. In the helping professions, this can lead to compassion fatigue; in executives, it can create distracting feelings of anxiety about people and circumstances that are beyond anyone's control. But those who protect themselves by deadening their feelings may lose touch with empathy. Empathic concern requires us to manage our personal distress without numbing ourselves to the pain of others. (See the sidebar "When Empathy Needs to Be Controlled.")

What's more, some lab research suggests that the appropriate application of empathic concern is critical to making moral judgments. Brain scans have revealed that when volunteers listened to tales of people subjected to physical pain, their own brain centers for experiencing such pain lit up instantly. But if the story was about psychological suffering, the higher brain centers involved in empathic concern and compassion took longer to activate. Some time is needed to grasp the psychological and moral dimensions of a situation. The more distracted we are, the less we can cultivate the subtler forms of empathy and compassion.

Building relationships

People who lack social sensitivity are easy to spot—at least for other people. They are the clueless among us. The CFO who is technically competent but bullies some people, freezes out

When Empathy Needs to Be Controlled

Getting a grip on our impulse to empathize with other people's feelings can help us make better decisions when someone's emotional flood threatens to overwhelm us.

Ordinarily, when we see someone pricked with a pin, our brains emit a signal indicating that our own pain centers are echoing that distress. But physicians learn in medical school to block even such automatic responses. Their attentional anesthetic seems to be deployed by the temporal-parietal junction and regions of the prefrontal cortex, a circuit that boosts concentration by tuning out emotions. That's what is happening in your brain when you distance yourself from others in order to stay calm and help them. The same neural network kicks in when we see a problem in an emotionally overheated environment and need to focus on looking for a solution. If you're talking with someone who is upset, this system helps you understand the person's perspective intellectually by shifting from the heart-to-heart of emotional empathy to the head-to-heart of cognitive empathy.

others, and plays favorites—but when you point out what he has just done, shifts the blame, gets angry, or thinks that you're the problem—is not trying to be a jerk; he's utterly unaware of his shortcomings.

Social sensitivity appears to be related to cognitive empathy. Cognitively empathic executives do better at overseas assignments, for instance, presumably because they quickly pick up implicit norms and learn the unique mental models of a new culture. Attention to social context lets us act with skill no matter what the situation, instinctively follow the universal algorithm for etiquette, and behave in ways that put others at ease. (In another age this might have been called good manners.)

Circuitry that converges on the anterior hippocampus reads social context and leads us intuitively to act differently with, say, our college buddies than with our families or our colleagues. In concert with the deliberative prefrontal cortex, it squelches the impulse to do something inappropriate. Accordingly, one brain test for sensitivity to context assesses the function of the hippocampus. The University of Wisconsin neuroscientist Richard Davidson hypothesizes that people who are most alert to social situations exhibit stronger activity and more connections between the hippocampus and the prefrontal cortex than those who just can't seem to get it right.

The same circuits may be at play when we map social networks in a group—a skill that lets us navigate the relationships in those networks well. People who excel at organizational influence can not only sense the flow of personal connections but also name the people whose opinions hold most sway, and so focus on persuading those who will persuade others.

Alarmingly, research suggests that as people rise through the ranks and gain power, their ability to perceive and maintain personal connections tends to suffer a sort of psychic attrition. In studying encounters between people of varying status, Dacher Keltner, a psychologist at Berkeley, has found that higher-ranking individuals consistently focus their gaze less on lower-ranking people and are more likely to interrupt or to monopolize the conversation.

In fact, mapping attention to power in an organization gives a clear indication of hierarchy: The longer it takes Person A to respond to Person B, the more relative power Person A has. Map response times across an entire organization, and you'll get a remarkably accurate chart of social standing. The boss leaves emails unanswered for hours; those lower down respond within minutes. This is so predictable that an algorithm for it—called automated social hierarchy detection—has been developed at Columbia University. Intelligence agencies reportedly are applying the algorithm to suspected terrorist gangs to piece together chains of influence and identify central figures.

But the real point is this: Where we see ourselves on the social ladder sets the default for how much attention we pay. This should be a warning to top executives, who need to respond to fast-moving competitive situations by tapping the full range of ideas and talents within an organization. Without a deliberate shift in attention, their natural inclination may be to ignore smart ideas from the lower ranks.

Focusing on the Wider World

Leaders with a strong outward focus are not only good listeners but also good questioners. They are visionaries who can sense the far-flung consequences of local decisions and imagine how the choices they make today will play out in the future. They are open to the surprising ways in which seemingly unrelated data can inform their central interests. Melinda Gates offered up a cogent example when she remarked on *60 Minutes* that her husband was the kind of person who would read an entire book about fertilizer. Charlie Rose asked, Why fertilizer? The connection was obvious to Bill Gates, who is constantly looking for technological advances that can save lives on a massive scale. "A few billion people would have to die if we hadn't come up with fertilizer," he replied.

Focusing on strategy

Any business school course on strategy will give you the two main elements: exploitation of your current advantage and exploration for new ones. Brain scans that were performed on 63 seasoned business decision makers as they pursued or switched between exploitative and exploratory strategies revealed the specific circuits involved. Not surprisingly, exploitation requires concentration on the job at hand, whereas exploration demands open awareness to recognize new possibilities. But exploitation is accompanied by activity in the brain's circuitry for anticipation and reward. In other words, it feels good to coast along in a familiar routine. When we switch to exploration, we have to make a deliberate cognitive effort to disengage from that routine in order to roam widely and pursue fresh paths.

What keeps us from making that effort? Sleep deprivation, drinking, stress, and mental overload all interfere with the executive circuitry used to make the cognitive switch. To sustain the outward focus that leads to innovation, we need some uninterrupted time in which to reflect and refresh our focus.

The wellsprings of innovation

In an era when almost everyone has access to the same information, new value arises from putting ideas together in novel ways and asking smart questions that open up untapped potential. Moments before we have a creative insight, the brain shows a third-of-a-second spike in gamma waves, indicating the synchrony of far-flung brain cells. The more neurons firing in sync, the bigger the spike. Its timing suggests that what's happening is the formation of a new neural network—presumably creating a fresh association.

But it would be making too much of this to see gamma waves as a secret to creativity. A classic model of creativity suggests how the various modes of attention play key roles. First we prepare our minds by gathering a wide variety of pertinent information, and then we alternate between concentrating intently on the problem and letting our minds wander freely. Those activities translate roughly into vigilance, when while immersing ourselves in all kinds of input, we remain alert for anything relevant to the problem at hand; selective attention to the specific creative challenge; and open awareness, in which we allow our minds to associate freely and the solution to emerge spontaneously. (That's why so many fresh ideas come to people in the shower or out for a walk or a run.)

The dubious gift of systems awareness

If people are given a quick view of a photo of lots of dots and asked to guess how many there are, the strong systems thinkers in the group tend to make the best estimates. This skill shows up in those who are good at designing software, assembly lines, matrix organizations, or interventions to save failing ecosystems— it's a very powerful gift indeed. After all, we live within extremely complex systems. But, suggests the Cambridge University psychologist Simon Baron-Cohen (a cousin of Sacha's), in a small but significant number of people, a strong systems awareness is coupled with an empathy deficit—a blind spot for what other people are thinking and feeling and for reading social situations. For that reason, although people with a superior systems understanding are organizational assets, they are not necessarily effective leaders.

An executive at one bank explained to me that it has created a separate career ladder for systems analysts so that they can progress in status and salary on the basis of their systems smarts alone. That way, the bank can consult them as needed while recruiting leaders from a different pool—one containing people with emotional intelligence.

Putting It All Together

For those who don't want to end up similarly compartmental-ized, the message is clear. A focused leader is not the person concentrating on the three most important priorities of the year, or the most brilliant systems thinker, or the one most in tune with the corporate culture. Focused leaders can command the full range of their own attention: They are in touch with their inner feelings, they can control their impulses, they are aware of how others see them, they understand what others need from them, they can weed out distractions and also allow their minds to roam widely, free of preconceptions.

This is challenging. But if great leadership were a paint-by-numbers exercise, great leaders would be more common. Prac-tically every form of focus can be strengthened. What it takes is not talent so much as diligence—a willingness to exercise the at-tention circuits of the brain just as we exercise our analytic skills and other systems of the body.

The link between attention and excellence remains hidden most of the time. Yet attention is the basis of the most essential of leadership skills—emotional, organizational, and strategic intelligence. And never has it been under greater assault. The constant onslaught of incoming data leads to sloppy shortcuts—triaging our email by reading only the subject lines, skipping many of our voice mails, skimming memos and reports. Not only do our habits of attention make us less effective, but the sheer volume of all those messages leaves us too little time to reflect on what they really mean. This was foreseen more than 40 years ago by the Nobel Prize–winning economist Herbert Simon. Information "consumes the attention of its recipients," he wrote in 1971. "Hence a wealth of information creates a poverty of attention."

My goal here is to place attention center stage so that you can direct it where you need it when you need it. Learn to master your attention, and you will be in command of where you, and your organization, focus.

Originally published in December 2013. Reprint R1312B

Nine Things Successful People Do Differently

by Heidi Grant

W hy have you been so successful in reaching some of your goals, but not others? If you aren't sure, you are far from alone in your confusion. It turns out that even brilliant, highly accomplished people are pretty lousy when it comes to understanding why they succeed or fail. The intuitive answer—that you are born predisposed to certain talents and lacking in others—is really just one small piece of the puzzle. In fact, decades of research on achievement suggest that successful people reach their goals not simply because of who they are but more often because of what they do.

1. Get Specific

When you set yourself a goal, try to be as specific as possible. "Lose five pounds" is a better goal than "lose some weight," because it gives you a clear idea of what success looks like. Knowing exactly what you want to achieve keeps you motivated until you get there. Also, think about the specific actions you need to take to reach your goal. Just promising you'll "eat less" or "sleep more" is too vague—be clear and precise. "I'll be in bed by 10 p.m. on weeknights" leaves no room for doubt about what you need to do, and whether or not you've actually done it.

2. Seize the Moment to Act on Your Goals

Given how busy most of us are, and how many goals we are juggling at once, it's not surprising that we routinely miss opportunities to act on a goal because we simply fail to notice them. Did you really have no time to work out today? No chance at any point to return that phone call? Achieving your goal means grabbing hold of these opportunities before they slip through your fingers.

To seize the moment, decide in advance when and where you will take each action you want to take. Again, be as specific as possible—for example, "If it's Monday, Wednesday, or Friday, I'll work out for 30 minutes before work." Studies show that this kind of planning will help your brain detect and seize the opportunity when it arises, increasing your chances of success by roughly 300%.

3. Know Exactly How Far You Have Left to Go

Achieving any goal requires honest and regular monitoring of your progress—if not by others, then by you yourself. If you don't know how well you are doing, you can't adjust your behavior or your strategies accordingly. Check your progress frequently—weekly, or even daily, depending on the goal.

Idea in Brief

The Problem

Success is not solely about inherent talent. If you're struggling to consistently achieve your goals, it may be time to take a new look at the habits and motivations that have gotten you this far—and where they might take you next.

The Solution

There are nine key behaviors you can adopt to more consistently achieve more of your goals. These behaviors include setting specific goals, monitoring progress, maintaining a positive mindset, seeking feedback, persisting through challenges, learning from failures, managing time effectively, and staying committed to your goals.

The Benefits

By reflecting on your behavior and adopting these practices, you can significantly improve your chances of achieving your objectives, boosting your personal and professional growth.

4. Be a Realistic Optimist

When you are setting a goal, by all means engage in lots of positive thinking about how likely you are to achieve it. Believing in your ability to succeed is enormously helpful for creating and sustaining your motivation. But whatever you do, don't underestimate how difficult it will be to reach your goal. Most goals worth achieving require time, planning, effort, and persistence. Studies show that assuming things will come to you easily and effortlessly leaves you ill-prepared for the journey ahead and significantly increases the odds of failure.

5. Focus on Getting Better Rather Than Being Good

Believing you have the ability to reach your goals is important, but so is believing you can *get* the ability. Many of us believe that our intelligence, personality, and physical aptitudes are fixed—that no matter what we do, we won't improve. As a result, we focus on goals that are all about proving ourselves rather than developing and acquiring new skills.

Fortunately, decades of research suggest that the belief in fixed ability is completely wrong—abilities of all kinds are profoundly malleable. Embracing the fact that you can change will allow you to make better choices and reach your fullest potential. People whose goals are about getting better, rather than being good, take difficulty in stride and appreciate the journey as much as the destination.

6. Have Grit

Grit is a willingness to commit to long-term goals and to persist in the face of difficulty. Studies show that gritty people obtain more education in their lifetime and earn higher college GPAs. Grit predicts which cadets will stick out their first grueling year at West Point. In fact, grit even predicts which round contestants will make it to at the Scripps National Spelling Bee.

The good news is, if you aren't particularly gritty now, you can do something about it. People who lack grit more often than not believe that they just don't have the innate abilities successful people have. If that describes your own thinking . . . well, there's no way to put this nicely: You are wrong. As I mentioned earlier, effort, planning, persistence, and good strategies are what it really takes to succeed. Embracing this knowledge will not only help you see yourself and your goals more accurately but also do wonders for your grit.

7. Build Your Willpower Muscle

Your self-control "muscle" is just like the other muscles in your body—when it doesn't get much exercise, it becomes weaker over time. But when you give it regular workouts by putting it to good use, it will grow stronger and stronger, and you will be better able to successfully reach your goals.

To build willpower, take on a challenge that requires you to do something you'd honestly rather not do: Give up high-fat snacks, do 100 sit-ups a day, stand up straight when you catch yourself slouching, or try to learn a new skill. When you find yourself wanting to give in, give up, or just not bother—don't. Start with just one activity, and make a plan for how you will deal with troubles when they occur: "If I have a craving for a snack, I will eat one piece of fresh fruit or three pieces of dried fruit." It will be hard in the beginning, but it will get easier, and that's the whole point. As your strength grows, you can take on more challenges and step up your self-control workout.

8. Don't Tempt Fate

No matter how strong your willpower muscle becomes, it's important to always respect the fact that it is limited, and if you overtax it, you will temporarily run out of steam. Don't try to take on two challenging tasks at once, if you can help it (such as quitting smoking and dieting at the same time). And don't put yourself in harm's way—many people are overly confident in their ability to resist temptation, and as a result they put themselves in situations where temptations abound. Successful people know not to make reaching a goal harder than it already is.

9. Focus on What You *Will* Do, Not What You *Won't* Do

Do you want to successfully lose weight, quit smoking, or put a lid on your bad temper? Then plan how you will replace bad habits with good ones, rather than focusing only on the bad habits themselves. Research on thought suppression (e.g., "Don't think about white bears!") has shown that trying to avoid a thought makes it even more active in your mind. The same holds true when it comes to behavior—by trying not to engage in a bad habit, our habits get strengthened rather than broken.

If you want to change your ways, ask yourself, "What will I do instead?" For example, if you are trying to gain control of your temper and stop flying off the handle, you might make a plan like, "If I am starting to feel angry, then I will take three deep breaths to calm down." By using deep breathing as a replacement for giving in to your anger, your bad habit will get worn away over time until it disappears completely.

. . .

It is my hope that, after reading about the nine things successful people do differently, you have gained some insight into the things you have been doing right all along. Even more important, I hope you are able to identify the mistakes that have derailed you and use that knowledge to your advantage from now on. Remember, you don't need to become a different person to become a more successful one. It's never what you are, but what you do.

Adapted from hbr.org, February 25, 2011. Reprint H006W2

2

The Right Way to Form New Habits

An interview with James Clear
by Alison Beard

EDITOR'S NOTE: We spoke with James Clear, entrepreneur and author of the book *Atomic Habits: An Easy and Proven Way to Build Good Habits and Break Bad Ones*, about why success requires discipline. It's something we've seen time and time again in the stories of great leaders. They might get up at 4 a.m. every day, read a book a week, or have a tried-and-true system for client outreach or interviewing.

Many of these people seem to have superhuman ambitions and work ethics. But there's another way of looking at their achievements: They've developed great habits. While most of us are slipping into bad habits—doing the easiest work first, making impulsive decisions, watching TV instead of studying a new idea, or even not getting enough sleep—high achievers are sticking to a plan and getting more out of their careers and lives as a result.

Whether your goal is to learn a new skill, finish a big project, or attend more networking events, Clear says there are simple and easy ways of developing better habits to help you get where you want to go.

Alison Beard: *At the taping of this interview, we're about to start a new year. For those of us who make New Year's resolutions and then quickly fail at sticking to them, how can we do better?*

James Clear: There are a lot of entry points to discussing habits through resolutions. So, I'll give you two. The first idea is that a lot of the time we start with goals or ambitions or resolutions that are really big, and simply scaling your habits down—or scaling those behaviors down—to something that's simple and easy to do is certainly a way to be more effective in the New Year, to increase the likelihood that you stick with your goal.

I refer to this as "the two-minute rule." You basically take whatever habit you're trying to build and scale it down to something that takes two minutes or less to do. So, "Read 30 books next year" becomes "Read one page a day." Or "Do yoga four days a week" becomes "Take out my yoga mat."

And sometimes people resist that a little, because they think, "OK, I know the real goal isn't just to take my yoga mat out each day. I know I actually want to do the workout." However, I think this is a deep truth about habits and certainly applies to New Year's resolutions too: The habit must be established before it can be improved. It has to become the standard in your life before you can worry about optimizing or scaling it up from there.

And then the second thing is to focus more on your identity than on the outcome. A lot of the discussion on New Year's resolutions is about how many books we want to read, or how much weight we want to lose, or how much more money we'd like to

Idea in Brief

The Problem
If you're struggling to learn a new skill or finish a large and complicated project, you may be focusing your effort in the wrong places. Success doesn't come from superhuman ambition and unrelenting work ethic. Success requires discipline and great habits.

The Solution
Instead of aiming for large, ambitious nebulous accomplishments, break down your goals into smaller, manageable actions. Focus on your desired identity rather than just the outcome you're looking for. Ask yourself: Who is the type of person that could achieve these outcomes?

The Benefits
Gradually building and reinforcing positive habits can shift your internal narrative and change your self-image. Small, consistent actions accumulate over time, leading to significant personal growth and sustainable long-term success.

earn next year, or whatever it is. But I think it's a useful question to ask yourself: "Who is the type of person that could achieve those outcomes?"

Who is the type of person who could lose 20 pounds, let's say? Well, maybe it's the type of person who doesn't miss workouts. And then your focus becomes building habits that reinforce that identity rather than achieving a particular outcome. And you can trust that the outcome will come naturally if you show up as a specific type of person each day.

It's funny you mention the identity piece of this. In the book, you write that we limit ourselves by saying things such as, "I'm not a morning person. I'm bad at remembering names. I'm always late. I'm not good with technology. I'm horrible at math."

And I almost laughed out loud when I read that because I say all of these things about myself even though I know that waking up earlier, remembering names, being on time, or getting better at math and technology would make me much better at my job as a business journalist. So how do I change that mindset about myself?

I think that perhaps the real reason that habits matter is that they can shift your internal narrative. They can change your self-image. And the first time you do something, or the 10th time, or maybe even the 100th time, you may not think differently about yourself yet or have adopted a new identity fully.

But at some point, when you keep showing up, you cross this invisible threshold and you start to think, "Hey, maybe I am a studious person," or "Maybe I am a clean and organized person after all."

Every action you take is like a vote for the type of person you want to become. And so, the more you show up and perform habits, the more you cast votes for being a certain type of person, the more you build up this body of evidence—the likelier you are to realize that, "Hey, this is who I actually am."

And I think this is what makes my approach a little bit different than what you often hear about behavior change, which is something like, "Fake it till you make it." "Fake it till you make it" is asking you to believe something positive about yourself without having evidence for it. And we have a word for beliefs that don't have evidence: We call them delusions.

At some point your brain doesn't like this mismatch between what you keep saying you are and what your behavior is. Behavior and beliefs are a two-way street, and my argument is that you should let the behavior lead the way. Start with one push-up. Start with writing one sentence. Start with meditating for one minute. Whatever it is.

Because, at least in that moment, you cannot deny that you were a writer, or you were the type of person who doesn't miss workouts, or you were a meditator. And in the long run that's the real objective. The goal's not to run a marathon. The goal is to become a runner. And once you start assigning those new identities to yourself, you're not even really pursuing behavior change anymore. You're just acting in alignment with the type of person you see yourself being. And so I think, in that way, true behavior change is really identity change.

How can we bring this into a work context? How have you seen bad habits derail people and the development of good habits really propel them forward?

So, specifically with work, I think we can broadly lump habits into two categories. The first category is what you might call *habits of energy*. For example, building good sleep habits. That's sort of a meta-habit; if you get that dialed in, you're in a better position to perform almost any other habit. And if you're not well rested, then you're kind of hindering yourself in your performance each day.

Pretty much any health-related habit falls in that bucket. Exercise, stress reduction, good nutrition habits, they're all in that habits-of-energy bucket. But the second category, and the one that is maybe more directly related to knowledge work, is what I would call *habits of attention*.

For almost all of us—and certainly for people who spend their time doing knowledge work or who are paid for the value of their creativity—the ideas you come up with are often a product of where you allocate your attention. So, what you read and what you consume often are the precursors to the thoughts you have, or to the creative or innovative ideas you come up with.

By improving your consumption habits, or your attention habits, you can dramatically improve the output you have at work. And we all live in this world with a fire hose of information. And so the ability to curate, to edit, to refine, to filter your information feed—whether that be the people you follow on [social media], the articles you read each day, the news sources you select, or the books you read—those are very important decisions that determine the downstream output. This is about what you're bringing in.

But there are also other habits you can build, the purpose of which is not to bring things in but to cut things out. It's to reduce the distractions. For example, one habit I've been following for the last year or so, which I probably do about 90% of days, is to leave my phone in another room until lunch each day.

I have a home office and if I bring my phone in with me and it's on the desk, I'm like everybody else: I'll check it every three minutes just because it's there. But if I leave it in another room, then it's only 30 seconds away, but I never go get it. And what's always so interesting to me is the question, Did I want it or not? In one sense, I did want it badly enough to check it every three minutes when it was next to me, but in another sense I never wanted it badly enough to walk the 30 seconds to go get it when I put it in another room.

And I think we see this so much with habits of technology and convenience and modern society—and particularly with smartphones or apps. Actions are so frictionless, so convenient, so simple, so easy that we find ourselves being pulled into them at the slightest whim. Just the faintest hint of desire is enough to pull us off course.

So if you can redesign your environment, whether it's your desk at work or your office at home or the kitchen counter, to make the actions of least resistance the good and productive ones, and increase the friction of the things that take your attention away, I think you will often find those habits of attention start to be allocated to more-productive areas. To recap, I would say that habits of energy and habits of attention are the two places to focus if you want to increase your work output.

What about habits of proactivity? Forcing yourself to do more sales calls or go to more networking events, that sort of thing?

Certainly being proactive is a really important part of life. I think it's a great quality to have. The language that you used about "forcing yourself" to do sales calls, or "forcing yourself" to go to networking events or whatever . . .

Motivating. Let's say "motivating."

Sure, OK. I do think that phrasing—"motivating"—is probably a better way to look at it. There are many ways to do this, or to accomplish the same outcome. And so, ask yourself questions like: What is the real goal here? What would this look like if it was easy? What is a way to achieve this that doesn't add friction to my life?

Those are important questions to ask and revisit, no matter what task you're trying to achieve. Because I think what most of us find, what is implicitly known, is that there are many behaviors that naturally pull us in, whether that's because they're attractive and convenient or because they just kind of naturally align with our personality or our strengths. There can be a variety of reasons. But focusing on those things that naturally pull you in, rather than things you have to push upon yourself, I think is generally the right approach to take.

As an example, you mentioned networking. Certainly having a strong network is a very powerful and important thing in the modern work environment. But for some people, if you feel more introverted, or you just don't gravitate toward chitchat or whatever, going to a networking event kind of sounds like a nightmare.

The good news is that we live in a time when there are actually many ways to network. The most effective networking strategy is to do great work and then share it publicly. And that could mean writing an interesting article; it could be recording a podcast or a video. Whatever it is, just do something interesting and then put that out into the world. It kind of becomes a magnet for people who are like-minded and interested in the same things. It becomes a much more powerful form of networking than going to a cocktail hour.

My point here is that by asking those questions (What is the real goal? What would this look like if it was easy? Is there a way to add this or do this or achieve this that would not bring friction into my life?), you often find that there are interesting alternative pathways for achieving a particular outcome.

Speaking of buckling down to write something or working on your most important project, what are some ways that you can encourage yourself to do that work first, to spend the most time on it?

There is a story in *Atomic Habits* about Twyla Tharp, a famous dance choreographer and instructor. She's a huge fan of habits and has had all these great routines throughout her career. For instance, she has this exercise routine that she does each morning, where she works out for two hours at the gym. But she always says the habit is not the training in the gym. The habit is hailing the cab outside her apartment.

And I think that's actually very instructive for anybody who's looking to do this kind of important work that you mention. How can I focus on the area of highest importance or the highest use of my time? And the answer is to make the habit the entry point, not the end point. View your habits as an entrance ramp to a highway.

What are the productive things that I should be spending time on? What are the highest-value tasks? Walk back the behavioral chain and try to find the tip of the spear. What is that entry point? And then if you can figure out what that first minute or two minutes look like, if you can automate that—the hailing of the cab for instance—then you find that the next chunk of time kind of falls into place automatically.

You write about how Victor Hugo developed a novel way of encouraging himself to sit down and work.

Hugo, a famous author, wrote a variety of books, and the story goes that when he signed the deal to write *The Hunchback of Notre Dame*, he got his advance and signed the contract and then did what a lot of us would do: He spent the next year procrastinating. He had friends over for dinner. He traveled. He went out to eat. He basically did everything except work on the book.

And this was before technology was there to distract him.

Right. I think maybe we just gravitate toward more fun and satisfying and entertaining uses of time, regardless of the time period.

Eventually, his publisher got wind of this and told him, "Dude, something has to change. Either you finish the book in six months or we're going to ask for the money back." Now he's facing this ultimatum, so Hugo brought his assistant into his chambers and they gathered up all his clothes and put them in this large chest, locked it up, and took it out of the house. And so all he was left with was this large shawl, this robe.

And suddenly, he had no clothes that were suitable for entertaining guests. No clothes that were suitable for traveling. No clothes that were suitable for going out to eat. He basically put himself on house arrest, and it worked. He wrote the book in five and a half months, and he handed it in two weeks early.

Now, in modern society, researchers would refer to that as a "commitment device." And I think commitment devices are powerful, because they can be methods for making habits more attractive. As another example, say that you go to bed tonight and you're thinking to yourself, "All right. Tomorrow's going to be the day. I'm going to wake up and I'm going to go for a run at six." And 6 a.m. rolls around and your bed is warm, it's cold outside and you think, "Maybe I'll just snooze instead."

But if you rewind the clock and go back a day and you text a friend and say, "Hey, let's meet at the park at 6:15 and go for a run," well, now 6 a.m. rolls around, and your bed is still warm, and it's still cold outside, but if you don't get up and go for a run, you're a jerk because you leave your friend at the park all alone. So, suddenly you have simultaneously made the habit of sleeping in less attractive and the habit of getting up and going for a run more attractive.

OK, so you've taken that first step. You're doing the easy entry point, ideally every morning. How do you build from there to more significant, visible progress?

At some point you want to graduate. This is what I call *habit graduation*. You want to step up to the next level. And my general rule of thumb is to try to get 1% better each day. The same way that money multiplies through compound interest, the effects of your habits multiply as you repeat them over time. I like to say habits are the compound interest of self-improvement.

Take reading, for example. Reading one book will not make you a genius. But if you build a habit of reading every day, then not only do you finish one book after another, but with each book you complete, you also have a new frame or a new way to view all the previous books you've read.

And the more connection points you have, the more perspectives you collect . . . that knowledge starts to compound on top of itself. A lot of habits are like that. Take doing an extra 10 minutes of work each day. Maybe that's one more sales call. Maybe it's one more email. Maybe it's just an extra 10 minutes to review the things you've written or revised, or to tweak or improve something.

Doing an extra 10 minutes on one day isn't much. But the difference between someone who doesn't do that and someone who does an extra 10 minutes every day over a 30-year career, that extra time can actually compound to a very surprising degree. That one extra sales call a day can mean a lot over the course of years and decades.

If you have good habits, time becomes your ally. You just need to be patient. You just need to let that compounding process work for you. But if you have bad habits, time becomes your enemy. And each day that clicks by, you dig the hole a little bit deeper, put yourself a little bit farther behind the eight ball.

That does make it sound, though, like it's just linear progression, and you argue very vehemently that it's not. There are going to be times when you stall, times when you regress. You talk about valleys and plateaus. So how do you navigate that emotionally and keep pressing on?

That's a really good point. The emotional part is a really true thing. You hear this a lot. I hear this from my readers a lot.

They'll say something like, "I've been running for a month, why can't I see a change in my body?" Or "I've been working on this novel for five and a half months now, the outline's still a mess. Is this thing ever going to be finished?"

When you're in the middle, when you're in the thick of the work, it's really easy to feel that way. And so sometimes I like to equate the process of building your habits to the process of heating up an ice cube. Let's say you walk into a room, and it's cold, like 25 degrees. You can see your breath and there's this ice cube sitting on the table in front of you. And you start to slowly heat the room up, 26, 27, 28 degrees. The ice cube is still sitting there. Then 29, 30, 31, and then you go from 31 to 32 degrees, and it's this one-degree shift that's no different from all the other one-degree shifts that came before it. But suddenly you hit this transition, and the ice cube melts.

The process of building better habits and getting better results is often like that. You're showing up each day, and the degrees are increasing a little bit. You're making these small improvements. You're getting 1% better. But you don't have the outcome that you're trying to achieve. Those delayed rewards haven't showed up yet.

So you feel like giving up, but giving up after doing a habit for a month or three months or six months is kind of like complaining about heating an ice cube from 25 to 31 degrees and it's not melting yet. The work is not being wasted, it's just being stored. And the willingness to stick with it is important.

I really like the San Antonio Spurs. They've won five NBA championships. They've got this quote hanging in their locker room that I think encapsulates this kind of philosophy well. It says something to the effect of, "Whenever I feel like giving up, I think about the stonecutter who takes his hammer and bangs on the rock 100 times without showing a crack. And then at the 101st blow it splits in two. And I know that it wasn't the 101st that did it, but all the 100 that came before."

I think that's exactly the kind of approach to take with your habits. It's not the last sentence that finishes the novel, it's all the ones that came before. It's not the last workout that gives you a fit body, it's all the ones that came before. And if you can be willing to keep showing up and keep hammering on the rock, to keep building up that potential energy, to know that it's not wasted, it's just being stored, then maybe you can start to fight that emotional battle of building better habits and ultimately get to the rewards you're waiting to accumulate.

I know you were an athlete, not a basketball player but a baseball player. Sports is obviously a place where people have to develop good habits and routines. You lift weights every day. You do get stronger over the long term. You hit 100 serves every day, you become more accurate. Even if you plateau or regress, you do sort of see that progress. But it seems much harder in a work context, where the correlation between the effort that you're putting in and then the achievement or reward is less clear.

The key insight here is that you want feedback to be visible and rapid. I think this is so important that in *Atomic Habits* I call it "the cardinal rule of behavior change." Which is this: Behaviors that are immediately rewarded get repeated. Behaviors that are immediately punished get avoided.

In sports, for example, as soon as you hit the serve, you immediately know if it was accurate or not. Is it in or is it out? That rapid feedback allows you to make an adjustment, hopefully a slight one, for the next time. And then you keep repeating that serve. You get this feedback almost instantly.

But in the modern work environment, particularly in large corporations, feedback is very delayed. It's kind of opaque. It's very difficult to see what your contribution is delivering to the bottom line or producing in terms of output.

I think one of the lessons to take away from this is that one of the most motivating feelings for the human brain is a feeling of progress. In the case of your own individual life you can decide what you want to track. This can take multiple forms. For my business, I do a weekly review where each Friday I track key metrics, revenue, expenses, profit, and so on.

My dad likes to swim, for example. Well, any day that he gets out of the pool, his body looks the same when he gets out of the water as it did when he got in. There's no visual feedback. So what he does is take out a little pocket calendar and put an "X" on that day. It's a very minor thing, but it is a signal of progress. It is a signal that he showed up and did the right thing that day.

I think it also reveals a lesson that probably a lot of managers or entrepreneurs can use as well, which is that you want the pace of feedback, the pace of measurement, to match the frequency of the habit.

And what if I have a big goal, like become a better manager? How do I distill that into smaller steps? The kind that you're talking about.

I would start by saying, "OK, I want to be a better manager. Great. That's a good vision. What does a better manager do? What do those daily behaviors look like? What sort of habits does a better manager have? Who is the type of person that could be a better manager?"

Then you start to elicit answers from yourself, such as, "Oh, a better manager gives praise each day." So maybe you build a habit of saying something positive to start off each team meeting. Or, "Oh, a better manager is a role model and models the behavior of the culture. We often talk about transparency, so now I need to build a habit of doing something transparent each day or each week, or in one-on-ones, or whatever. Maybe I start each one-on-one by sharing something about my personal life so that I'm vulnerable first and then my employees follow my lead." You get my point. You start to see which behaviors the identity [of a better manager] is associated with, and then you have something more concrete that you can focus on. You can focus on building those habits rather than being stuck in this high-level meta-mode where you think, "Well, I just really want to be a better manager" but that's very hard to translate into something practical.

So, why is it that good habits seem so hard to form yet easy to break and bad habits seem so easy to form and hard to break?

I thought about this a lot when I was working on *Atomic Habits* because I think, actually, asking that question can reveal a lot about what we want to do to build a good habit or to break a bad one.

Let's say we want to build good habits. Well, how come bad habits stick so readily? What you find is that they have a variety of qualities. The first quality that bad habits often have is that they're very obvious. For example, let's say that eating at fast-food restaurants is a bad habit or a habit that you don't want to perform as much.

Well, in America it's hard to drive down the street for more than 15 minutes without passing at least a few, if not a dozen, fast-food restaurants. They're very obvious. They're very prevalent in the environment. So that's a lesson that we can take and apply to our good habits. If you want a good habit to stick, then you should make it a big part of your environment.

Another quality that bad habits often have is that they're incredibly convenient. They're very frictionless. The incredible convenience of many bad habits is a big reason why we stick to them so much. So if you want your good habits to stick, they need to be as easy and convenient as possible.

Another quality of bad habits is that the benefit is usually immediate and the cost is usually delayed. And with good habits it's often the reverse. So the benefit of going to the gym for a week is not a whole lot. If anything, your body's sore. You haven't really changed. You look the same in the mirror. The scale is roughly the same. It's only if you stick to that habit for a year or two or three that you get the outcome you want.

So there's this gap. There's sort of this valley of death in the beginning with a lot of good habits. You start doing them, but you don't have the immediate rewards that you're showing up and hoping you get. Whereas with bad habits there's this mismatch between the immediate outcome that you get ("Hey this feels great in the moment, I should do this") and then it turns out that it ultimately hurts you in the long run.

The cost of your good habits is in the present. The cost of your bad habits is in the future. A lot of the reason why bad habits form so readily and good habits are so unlikely, or resistant to form, has to do with that gap in time and reward.

Adapted from *HBR IdeaCast* podcast, episode 716, December 31, 2019.

Use a 10-Minute Diary to Stay on Track

by Teresa M. Amabile and Steven J. Kramer

What's the best way to use the last 10 minutes of your day? Many productivity gurus recommend an end-of-the-day meeting with yourself to review your to-do list, check how you're doing against short- and long-term goals, or select the most challenging project you'll tackle the following day. Our research suggests that not only should you do an end-of-day review, but you'll reap the greatest benefits for your productivity and personal well-being if you actually record your thoughts in a "mini-diary." A work diary will improve your focus, track your progress, and make you more satisfied with your work—which will help you be even more productive.

No question: This reflective time is often the first thing that we drop when we're feeling overloaded. Adding a daily writing assignment—the word "diary" conjures up a long-term commitment—seems counterproductive to making headway on "real" work. So try it for just one month, focusing on just one short-term project (for example, developing a departmental staffing plan), or just one area of professional development (improving your presentation skills).

Take 10 minutes at the end of each workday, write no more than 100 words, and see what you've learned after four weeks. You may be surprised.

You'll get five benefits from keeping a work diary. You:

1. *Track your progress.* The diary is a record of your "small wins," incremental steps toward meaningful goals, that can boost your motivation—if only you take a moment to reflect on them.

2. *Plan.* You use the diary as a tool for drafting your next steps toward the goal.

3. *Fuel personal growth.* The diary gives you a way of working through your difficult—even traumatic—work events, gaining new perspectives on them.

4. *Sharpen your focus.* You identify your strengths, passions, and challenges by looking at patterns in your entries over time. For example, your diary may reveal that you've been spending a lot of time on low-priority issues. Reviewing your diary and identifying this pattern can help you recommit to focusing your time and energy on your most important work.

5. *Develop patience.* The diary serves as a reminder during frustrating days that, in the past, you've persevered through days that, at the time, seemed even worse—and that you have still made progress over time.

Our research shows that, of all these benefits, using a work diary to track your progress may be the most important one

Idea in Brief

The Problem

High performers have full calendars—and full plates. The more you do and do well, the more demands people place on you. You excel at your job and push yourself to continue to learn and grow, but sometimes it's hard to keep track of your progress on your short- and long-term goals.

The Solution

Take 10 minutes at the end of your day to record the small successes you had and to make a plan for the next few days. Focus on one event or insight from the day, write no more than 100 words, and use whatever tools (app, notebook) work for you.

The Benefits

Tracking your daily progress in a work diary will improve your focus and productivity and increase your job satisfaction. You'll feel highly motivated to dig into your work even during stressful periods of overload and uncertainty.

for your productivity and psychological well-being. As part of a massive study on the psychology of everyday work life, we collected nearly 12,000 diary entries from 238 professionals working on complex, creative projects. Our analyses revealed a big surprise. Of all the things that could make people feel both happy and highly motivated to dig into their work, the single most important event was simply making progress in work they cared about. We call this *the progress principle*, and it applies even when the progress is a small win. When we see we're making progress, we're motivated to keep going, and it's easier to keep our focus—even when we encounter setbacks. Witness this example, from the diary of a software engineer in our study:

> *Today, when I started work [. . .] there was a note from a user regarding some work I had done for him. It was very*

complimentary and it made me feel pretty good. Also in the note was a request to go ahead with an enhancement to the database analysis package. I was able to code and load this request today in less than the estimated time, which makes me feel good. And I know it will please our user when he comes in tomorrow.

That entry probably took fewer than five minutes to write. Yet, at the end of the day, that engineer was quite happy—and seems motivated toward high productivity the next day, too. Making progress, and noting it, can provide a real lift—and give you the boost you need to keep working on the projects that will yield the greatest benefit for your organization and its customers.

Daily writing and review helps in negative situations, too. In the following entry, an employee struggles to gain a sense of control during a traumatic event in her company—a downsizing. Even though her own job might still be in jeopardy, her work diary helps her shape a healthy perspective; it enables her to focus on her work, amid swirling gossip and uncertainty. Her personal growth is almost palpable in this entry:

This morning, my project manager came over and sat next to me and asked me if I was OK after all the layoffs that went on yesterday. I thought that was really nice. We all had a very rough day yesterday, but I feel better today. In 45 days, we will all know our fate, and then we can get on with our lives one way or the other. The outcome of all this is really out of our control. I'm trying to concentrate on what IS in my control, by doing my job.

And here, in his final entry for our study, a professional tells us directly how valuable it was for him to fill out the diary questionnaire that we sent every day during his project:

> *I did find value in doing the questionnaires, especially when I was disciplined enough to do them at the end of the day, when everything was still fresh in my mind. It helped me to reflect on the day, my accomplishments, the team's work, and how I was feeling in general. When you're working at a hectic pace, reflection time is rare, but [it's] really beneficial.*

Don't dismiss the idea of trying a work diary because you think you have to create finely-crafted entries for posterity. We've found that if you avoid making a big commitment to it, you'll be more successful. Don't worry about how to express yourself. Simply describe one event or insight from the day. In our study, the average length of the entries was a mere 54 words.

To get started:

- *Pick a time.* Consider when you're most likely to have ten minutes to yourself. Ideally, this will be the same time each day, because it's much easier to get into the habit that way. For some of us, that will be the very end of the day, just before bed. For others, it's at the end of the workday, or on the train ride home.

- *Create a memory trigger.* Choose something you'll see or hear at the designated writing time. For example, if you want to do the diary before you end your workday, set a repeating alarm in your calendar for 10 minutes before your usual quitting time. If you choose bedtime, put your diary and a pen on your bedside table.

- *Select a medium.* Find something you enjoy using. People have very different preferences for diarykeeping. Some love a leather-bound, monogrammed, silk-bookmarked, five-year diary, with just a few pre-ruled lines for each day. Others like electronic journaling using one of the many apps or online programs available. Whether it's a Word doc, a diary app, a spiral-bound notebook, an elegant journal, or an Excel spreadsheet, use whatever works for you.

- *Reflect on your day.* Some people discover what they think as they write, but most of us need a bit of time to collect our thoughts. Use the first three minutes to let your mind go to any one of these types of events from the day:

  - Progress . . . and what led to it. (Congratulate yourself!)

  - Setbacks . . . and what might have caused them. (Learn from them!)

  - Something good. (Feel grateful!)

  - Something difficult. (Get it off your chest!)

  - One thing you can do tomorrow to make your work go better. (Then plan how to do it!)

  - Anything else that dominates your reflection time.

- *Write.* Use the remaining seven minutes to jot down your thoughts. Don't worry about grammar, proper sentence construction, style, etc. Focus on the event.

- *Review.* Once in a while, take a few minutes to sit down with your journal and a favorite beverage in a comfy chair. Much of the value in a diary comes from periodically reviewing the past few days (or more).

Keep a diary for just one project, for just a few weeks, and you might find it's a productivity tool you don't want to give up.

Adapted from *HBR Guide to Getting the Right Work Done*. Product 1153

3

How to Play to Your Strengths

by Laura Morgan Roberts, Gretchen M. Spreitzer, Jane E. Dutton, Robert E. Quinn, Emily Heaphy, and Brianna Barker Caza

Most feedback accentuates the negative. During formal employee evaluations, discussions invariably focus on "opportunities for improvement," even if the overall evaluation is laudatory. Informally, the sting of criticism lasts longer than the balm of praise. Multiple studies have shown that people pay keen attention to negative information. For example, when asked to recall important emotional events, people remember four negative memories for every positive one. No wonder most executives give and receive performance reviews with all the enthusiasm of a child on the way to the dentist.

Traditional, corrective feedback has its place, of course; every organization must filter out failing employees and ensure that everyone performs at an expected level of competence.

Unfortunately, feedback that ferrets out flaws can lead otherwise talented managers to overinvest in shoring up or papering over their perceived weaknesses, or forcing themselves onto an ill-fitting template. Ironically, such a focus on problem areas prevents companies from reaping the best performance from its people. After all, it's a rare baseball player who is equally good at every position. Why should a natural third baseman labor to develop his skills as a right fielder?

The alternative, as the Gallup Organization researchers Marcus Buckingham, Donald Clifton, and others have suggested, is to foster excellence in the third baseman by identifying and harnessing his unique strengths. It is a paradox of human psychology that while people remember criticism, they respond to praise. The former makes them defensive and therefore unlikely to change, while the latter produces confidence and the desire to perform better. Managers who build up their strengths can reach their highest potential. This positive approach does not pretend to ignore or deny the problems that traditional feedback mechanisms identify. Rather, it offers a separate and unique feedback experience that counterbalances negative input. It allows managers to tap into strengths they may or may not be aware of and so contribute more to their organizations.

During the past few years, we have developed a powerful tool to help people understand and leverage their individual talents. Called the Reflected Best Self (RBS) exercise, our method allows managers to develop a sense of their "personal best" in order to increase their future potential. The RBS exercise is but one example of new approaches springing from an area of research called positive organizational scholarship (POS). Just as psychologists know that people respond better to praise than to criticism, organizational behavior scholars are finding that when

Idea in Brief

The Problem

Most feedback accentuates the negative. During formal employee evaluations, discussions invariably focus on "opportunities for improvement," even if the overall evaluation is laudatory. No wonder most executives—and their direct reports—dread them.

Traditional, corrective feedback has its place, of course; every organization must filter out failing employees and ensure that everyone performs at an expected level of competence. But too much emphasis on problem areas prevents companies from reaping the best from their people. After all, it's a rare baseball player who is equally good at every position. Why should a natural third baseman labor to develop his skills as a right fielder?

The Solution

This article presents a tool to help you understand and leverage your strengths. Called the Reflected Best Self (RBS) exercise, it offers a unique feedback experience that counterbalances negative input. It allows you to tap into talents you may or may not be aware of and so increase your career potential.

To begin the RBS exercise, you first need to solicit comments from family, friends, colleagues, and teachers, asking them to give specific examples of times in which those strengths were particularly beneficial. Next, you need to search for common themes in the feedback, organizing them in a table to develop a clear picture of your strong suits. Third, you must write a self-portrait—a description of yourself that summarizes and distills the accumulated information. And finally, you need to redesign your personal job description to build on what you're good at.

The Benefits

The RBS exercise will help you discover who you are at the top of your game. Once you're aware of your best self, you can shape the positions you choose to play—both now and in the next phase of your career.

companies focus on positive attributes such as resilience and trust, they can reap impressive bottom-line returns. (For more on this research, see the sidebar "The Positive Organization.") Thousands of executives, as well as tomorrow's leaders enrolled in business schools around the world, have completed the RBS exercise.

In this article, we will walk you through the RBS exercise step-by-step and describe the insights and results it can yield. Before we proceed, however, a few caveats are in order. First, understand that the tool is not designed to stroke your ego; its purpose is to assist you in developing a plan for more effective action. (Without such a plan, you'll keep running in place.) Second, the lessons generated from the RBS exercise can elude you if you don't pay sincere attention to them. If you are too burdened by time pressures and job demands, you may just file the information away and forget about it. To be effective, the exercise requires commitment, diligence, and follow-through. It may even be helpful to have a coach keep you on task. Third, it's important to conduct the RBS exercise at a different time of year than the traditional performance review so that negative feedback from traditional mechanisms doesn't interfere with the results of the exercise.

Used correctly, the RBS exercise can help you tap into unrecognized and unexplored areas of potential. Armed with a constructive, systematic process for gathering and analyzing data about your best self, you can burnish your performance at work.

Step 1: Identify Respondents and Ask for Feedback

The first task in the exercise is to collect feedback from a variety of people inside and outside work. By gathering input from a variety of sources—family members, past and present colleagues,

The Positive Organization

Positive organizational scholarship (POS) is an area of organizational behavior research that focuses on the positive dynamics (such as strength, resilience, vitality, trust, and so on) that lead to positive effects (like improved productivity and performance) in individuals and organizations. The word "positive" refers to the discipline's affirmative bias, "organizational" focuses on the processes and conditions that occur in group contexts, and "scholarship" reflects the rigor, theory, scientific procedures, and precise definition in which the approach is grounded.

The premise of POS research is that by understanding the drivers of positive behavior in the workplace, organizations can rise to new levels of achievement. For example, research by Marcial Losada and Emily Heaphy at the University of Michigan suggests that when individuals or teams hear five positive comments to every negative one, they unleash a level of positive energy that fuels higher levels of individual and group performance. Kim Cameron, a POS researcher, has demonstrated how this positive approach has helped the workers at Rocky Flats, a nuclear site in Colorado, tackle difficult and dangerous work in record time. Begun in 1995 and estimated to take 70 years and $36 billion, the Rocky Flats cleanup project is now slated for completion in ten years, with a price tag of less than $7 billion. Kaiser-Hill, the company in charge of the cleanup, replaced a culture of denial with one that fostered employee flexibility and celebrated achievements. The result was that employees developed new procedures that were fast, smart, and safe.

POS does not adopt one particular theory or framework but draws from the full spectrum of organizational theories to explain and predict high performance. To that end, a core part of the POS mission is to create cases, tools, and assessments that can help organizations improve their practices. The Reflected Best Self exercise is just one example of the kinds of practice tools available from POS. (For more information about POS, see the University of Michigan's website at https://positiveorgs.bus.umich.edu/.)

friends, teachers, and so on—you can develop a much broader and richer understanding of yourself than you can from a standard performance evaluation.

As we describe the process of the Reflected Best Self exercise, we will highlight the experience of Robert Duggan (not his real name), whose self-discovery process is typical of the managers we've observed. Having retired from a successful career in the military at a fairly young age and earned an MBA from a top business school, Robert accepted a midlevel management position at an IT services firm. Despite strong credentials and leadership experience, Robert remained stuck in the same position year after year. His performance evaluations were generally good but not strong enough to put him on the high-potential track. Disengaged, frustrated, and disheartened, Robert grew increasingly stressed and disillusioned with his company. His workday felt more and more like an episode of *Survivor*.

Seeking to improve his performance, Robert enrolled in an executive education program and took the RBS exercise. As part of the exercise, Robert gathered feedback from 11 individuals from his past and present who knew him well. He selected a diverse but balanced group—his wife and two other family members, two friends from his MBA program, two colleagues from his time in the army, and four current colleagues.

Robert then asked these individuals to provide information about his strengths, accompanied by specific examples of moments when Robert used those strengths in ways that were meaningful to them, to their families or teams, or to their organizations. Many people—Robert among them—feel uncomfortable asking for exclusively positive feedback, particularly from colleagues. Accustomed to hearing about their strengths and weaknesses simultaneously, many executives imagine

Requesting Feedback

Here's some sample language to use as you solicit feedback from family, friends, teachers, and colleagues.

Dear Colleague,

I'm currently working on creating a personal development plan. As part of that process, I'm gathering feedback from a variety of people I work with closely to help me develop a broader understanding of the strengths I bring to our work. I'm hoping you'll be willing to share your thoughts with me.

From your perspective, what would you say my professional strengths are? Just two or three would be helpful, and if you could cite specific examples of situations where I used those in ways that were meaningful to you, that would be great. Your candid feedback and examples will help me shape my development plan.

Thank you for taking the time to help me.
Sincerely,
X

any positive feedback will be unrealistic, even false. Some also worry that respondents might construe the request as presumptuous or egotistical. But once managers accept that the exercise will help them improve their performance, they tend to dive in.

Within 10 days, Robert received email responses from all 11 people describing specific instances when he had made important contributions—including pushing for high quality under a tight deadline, being inclusive in communicating with a diverse group, and digging for critical information. The answers he received surprised him. As a military veteran and a technical person holding an MBA, Robert rarely yielded to his

Gathering Feedback

A critical step in the Reflected Best Self exercise involves soliciting feedback from family, friends, teachers, and colleagues. Email is an effective way of doing this, not only because it's comfortable and fast but also because it's easy to cut and paste responses into an analysis table such as the one in the main body of this article.

Below is the feedback Robert, a manager we observed, received from a current colleague and from a former coworker in the army.

From: Amy Chen
To: Robert Duggan
Subject: Re: Request for feedback

Dear Robert,

One of the greatest ways that you add value is that you stand for doing the right thing. For example, I think of the time that we were behind on a project for a major client and quality began to slip. You called a meeting and suggested that we had a choice: We could either pull a C by satisfying the basic requirements, or we could pull an A by doing excellent work. You reminded us that we could contribute to a better outcome. In the end, we met our deadline, and the client was very happy with the result.

From: Mike Bruno
To: Robert Duggan
Subject: Re: Request for feedback

One of the greatest ways you add value is that you persist in the face of adversity. I remember the time that we were both leading troops under tight security. We were getting conflicting information from the ground and from headquarters. You pushed to get the ground and HQ folks to talk to each other despite the tight time pressure. That information saved all of our lives. You never lost your calm, and you never stopped expecting or demanding the best from everyone involved.

emotions. But in reading story after story from his respondents, Robert found himself deeply moved—as if he were listening to appreciative speeches at a party thrown in his honor. The stories were also surprisingly convincing. He had more strengths than he knew. (For more on step 1, refer to the sidebars "Requesting Feedback" and "Gathering Feedback.")

Step 2: Recognize Patterns

In this step, Robert searched for common themes among the feedback, adding to the examples with observations of his own, then organizing all the input into a table. (To view parts of Robert's table, see the exhibit "Finding common themes.") Like many who participate in the RBS exercise, Robert expected that, given the diversity of respondents, the comments he received would be inconsistent or even competing. Instead, he was struck by their uniformity. The comments from his wife and family members were similar to those from his army buddies and work colleagues. Everyone took note of Robert's courage under pressure, high ethical standards, perseverance, curiosity, adaptability, respect for diversity, and team-building skills. Robert suddenly realized that even his small, unconscious behaviors had made a huge impression on others. In many cases, he had forgotten about the specific examples cited until he read the feedback, because his behavior in those situations had felt like second nature to him.

The RBS exercise confirmed Robert's sense of himself, but for those who are unaware of their strengths, the exercise can be truly illuminating. Edward, for example, was a recently minted MBA executive in an automotive firm. His colleagues and subordinates were older and more experienced than he, and he felt

Finding common themes

Creating a table helps you make sense of the feedback you collect. By clustering examples, you can more easily compare responses and identify common themes.

Common theme	Examples given	Possible interpretation
Ethics, values, and courage	• I take a stand when superiors and peers cross the boundaries of ethical behavior. • I am not afraid to stand up for what I believe in. I confront people who litter or who yell at their kids in public.	I am at my best when I choose the harder right over the easier wrong. I derive even more satisfaction when I am able to teach others. I am professionally courageous.
Curiosity and perseverance	• I gave up a promising career in the military to get my MBA. • I investigated and solved a security breach through an innovative approach.	• I like meeting new challenges. • I take risks and persevere despite obstacles.
Ability to build teams	• In high school, I assembled a team of students that helped improve the school's academic standards. • I am flexible and willing to learn from others, and I give credit where credit is due.	• I thrive when working closely with others.

uncomfortable disagreeing with them. But he learned through the RBS exercise that his peers appreciated his candid alternative views and respected the diplomatic and respectful manner with which he made his assertions. As a result, Edward grew bolder in making the case for his ideas, knowing that his boss and colleagues listened to him, learned from him, and appreciated what he had to say.

Other times, the RBS exercise sheds a more nuanced light on the skills one takes for granted. Beth, for example, was a lawyer who negotiated on behalf of nonprofit organizations. Throughout her life, Beth had been told she was a good listener, but her exercise respondents noted that the interactive, empathetic, and insightful manner in which she listened made her particularly effective. The specificity of the feedback encouraged Beth to take the lead in future negotiations that required delicate and diplomatic communications.

For naturally analytical people, the analysis portion of the exercise serves both to integrate the feedback and develop a larger picture of their capabilities. Janet, an engineer, thought she could study her feedback as she would a technical drawing of a suspension bridge. She saw her "reflected best self" as something to interrogate and improve. But as she read the remarks from family, friends, and colleagues, she saw herself in a broader and more human context. Over time, the stories she read about her enthusiasm and love of design helped her rethink her career path toward more managerial roles in which she might lead and motivate others.

Step 3: Compose Your Self-Portrait

The next step is to write a description of yourself that summarizes and distills the accumulated information. The description should weave themes from the feedback together with your self-observations into a composite of who you are at your best. The self-portrait is not designed to be a complete psychological and cognitive profile. Rather, it should be an insightful image that you can use as a reminder of your previous contributions and as a guide for future action. The portrait itself should not be a set of bullet points but rather a prose composition beginning with the phrase, "When I am at my best, I . . ." The process of writing out a two- to four-paragraph narrative cements the image of your best self in your consciousness. The narrative form also helps you draw connections between the themes in your life that may previously have seemed disjointed or unrelated. Composing the portrait takes time and demands careful consideration, but at the end of this process, you should come away with a rejuvenated image of who you are.

In developing his self-portrait, Robert drew on the actual words that others used to describe him, rounding out the picture with his own sense of himself at his best. He excised competencies that felt off the mark. This didn't mean he discounted them, but he wanted to assure that the overall portrait felt authentic and powerful. "When I am at my best," Robert wrote,

> *I stand by my values and can get others to understand why doing so is important. I choose the harder right over the easier wrong. I enjoy setting an example. When I am in learning mode and am curious and passionate about a project, I can work intensely and untiringly. I enjoy taking things on that others might be afraid of or see as too difficult. I'm able to set limits and find alternatives when a current approach is not working. I don't always assume that I am right or know best, which engenders respect from others. I try to empower and give credit to others. I am tolerant and open to differences.*

As Robert developed his portrait, he began to understand why he hadn't performed his best at work: He lacked a sense of mission. In the army, he drew satisfaction from the knowledge that the safety of the men and women he led, as well as the nation he served, depended on the quality of his work. He enjoyed the sense of teamwork and variety of problems to be solved. But as an IT manager in charge of routine maintenance on new hardware products, he felt bored and isolated from other people.

The portrait-writing process also helped Robert create a more vivid and elaborate sense of what psychologists would call his "possible self"—not just the person he is in his day-to-day job but the person he might be in completely different contexts. Organizational researchers have shown that when we develop a sense of our best possible self, we are better able make positive changes in our lives.

Step 4: Redesign Your Job

Having pinpointed his strengths, Robert's next step was to redesign his personal job description to build on what he was good at. Given the fact that routine maintenance work left him cold, Robert's challenge was to create a better fit between his work and his best self. Like most RBS participants, Robert found that the strengths the exercise identified could be put into play in his current position. This involved making small changes in the way he worked, in the composition of his team, and in the way he spent his time. (Most jobs have degrees of freedom in all three of these areas; the trick is operating within the fixed constraints of your job to redesign work at the margins, allowing you to better play to your strengths.)

Robert began by scheduling meetings with systems designers and engineers who told him they were having trouble getting timely information flowing between their groups and Robert's maintenance team. If communication improved, Robert believed, new products would not continue to be saddled with the serious and costly maintenance issues seen in the past. Armed with a carefully documented history of those maintenance problems as well as a new understanding of his naturally analytical and creative team-building skills, Robert began meeting regularly with the designers and engineers to brainstorm better ways to prevent problems with new products. The meetings satisfied two of Robert's deepest best-self needs: He was interacting with more people at work, and he was actively learning about systems design and engineering.

Robert's efforts did not go unnoticed. Key executives remarked on his initiative and his ability to collaborate across functions, as well as on the critical role he played in making new products more reliable. They also saw how he gave credit to others. In less than nine months, Robert's hard work paid off, and he was promoted to program manager. In addition to receiving more pay and higher visibility, Robert enjoyed his work more. His passion was reignited; he felt intensely alive and authentic. Whenever he felt down or lacking in energy, he reread the original email feedback he had received. In difficult situations, the email messages helped him feel more resilient.

Robert was able to leverage his strengths to perform better, but there are cases in which RBS findings conflict with the realities of a person's job. This was true for James, a sales executive who told us he was "in a world of hurt" over his work situation. Unable to meet his ambitious sales goals, tired of flying around the globe to fight fires, his family life on the verge of collapse, James had suffered enough. The RBS exercise revealed that James was at his best when managing people and leading change, but these natural skills did not and could not come into play in his current job. Not long after he did the exercise, he quit his high-stress position and started his own successful company.

Other times, the findings help managers aim for undreamed-of positions in their own organizations. Sarah, a high-level administrator at a university, shared her best-self portrait with key colleagues, asking them to help her identify ways to better exploit her strengths and talents. They suggested that she would be an ideal candidate for a new executive position. Previously, she would never have considered applying for the job, believing herself unqualified. To her surprise, she handily beat out the other candidates.

Beyond Good Enough

We have noted that while people remember criticism, awareness of faults doesn't necessarily translate into better performance. Based on that understanding, the RBS exercise helps you remember your strengths—and construct a plan to build on them. Knowing your strengths also offers you a better understanding of how to deal with your weaknesses—and helps you gain the confidence you need to address them. It allows you to say, "I'm great at leading but lousy at numbers. So rather than teach me remedial math, get me a good finance partner." It also allows you to be clearer in addressing your areas of weakness as a manager. When Tim, a financial services executive, received feedback that he was a great listener and coach, he also became more aware that he had a tendency to spend too much time being a cheerleader and too little time keeping his employees to task. Susan, a senior advertising executive, had the opposite problem: While her feedback lauded her results-oriented management approach, she wanted to be sure that she hadn't missed opportunities to give her employees the space to learn and make mistakes.

In the end, the strength-based orientation of the RBS exercise helps you get past the "good enough" bar. Once you discover who you are at the top of your game, you can use your strengths to better shape the positions you choose to play—both now and in the next phase of your career.

Originally published in January 2005. Reprint R0501G

Get the Actionable Feedback You Need to Get Promoted

by Sabina Nawaz

Tamara joined her company as a group manager. Her deep technical skills, competence in managing people, and ability to deliver results helped her get rapidly promoted to vice president. Tamara was well regarded by the executive team at her company, many of whom continued to encourage her professional advancement. In her organization, several of her peers had been promoted to the next level within three years. After her third year as VP, Tamara asked her manager what it would take for her to get promoted again. Her manager said, "You need to be more strategic." When Tamara pushed for more specifics, he said, "I'll point it out next time I notice it."

After a couple of months with no feedback, Tamara asked her manager for direct feedback as she walked with him after a meeting where she had presented. Her manager said, "You were not speaking at the right altitude." Frustrated with the lack of actionable feedback, Tamara came to our next coaching session feeling stuck about how to get more-specific feedback from her manager.

Tamara is not alone. When you rise up the executive ranks, one of the commodities in scarce supply is actionable feedback from those you report to. An occasional fat bonus or raise fills in the blanks for positive feedback, whereas being assigned to "special" projects—projects that go nowhere—might signal it's time to move on. What you need to grow as a leader is the ability to course correct on the fly. You need consistent, actionable feedback.

Useful feedback is hard to come by because most managers aren't clear what feedback is actionable or think that, as an executive, you have the seniority to translate their high-level edict into behavioral changes. In other instances, they may simply be too preoccupied with other priorities or projects that are on fire rather than something you're working on.

How do you make sure you get feedback that you can use to become a better leader? Here are five ways to solicit concrete, specific observations that can result in being promoted faster:

- *Be proactive.* Get the feedback you need by asking for it and scheduling a time to receive it. Most people will say yes when asked if they'd be willing to provide feedback, but despite their best intentions, very few follow up. So set a specific time and place to initiate the conversation. For example, carve out time by adding feedback as an agenda item for a monthly meeting. This frees your manager from the burden of having to remember to follow up and allows them to focus on what's most important: their comments. And by initiating the conversation and following through at the appointed time, you're signaling that you're serious about getting their input and improving yourself.

Idea in Brief

The Problem

The higher you rise through the ranks, the more you develop a reputation as a high performer, and the less likely you are to receive meaningful, actionable feedback that helps you grow and continue to expand your abilities and influence.

The Solution

To take in high-level directives and translate them into behavior changes that will help you build skills and continue to perform at your highest level, you must gather better feedback. Be proactive and seek that feedback by posing questions that require specific answers, probing your manager for detailed and actionable responses, digging into compliments for deeper insights, and listening to criticism with grace.

The Benefits

By taking these steps to obtain detailed observations and specific examples, you'll identify areas to focus on improving, discover opportunities to foster personal growth, and enhance your overall effectiveness as a leader.

- *Ask questions that require specific answers.* During the conversation, avoid generic assurances by asking questions that elicit specific information. Instead of saying, "Do you have feedback for me?" try something like, "What did you notice at our meeting yesterday when I was framing the topic? What's one thing I did well? What's one thing I should do more of or change?" Avoid questions that can easily yield a yes or no response. Give your boss lots of room to choose how they answer and something concrete to respond to. End with a question such as, "Is there anything else?" At this point in the conversation, you've already warmed up the feedback provider and may receive more valuable insights.

- *Guide your manager to a specific response.* Have you ever asked for and received feedback, only to feel frustrated when you don't know how to implement it? For instance, your manager might tell you, "The one thing I liked the most in our last meeting was that you framed the topic strategically." It's helpful to know that you were viewed as strategic, but it's harder to understand what you need to replicate to be viewed as strategic again by that comment alone. Probe for specific behaviors to better understand what your manager means: "What did I say or do that made my framing strategic?" Now they might say, "You started by making a comparison between the competitive landscape and the customer's problem. Then you tied those takeaways to the corporate strategic pillars. I noticed that made the senior vice president sit forward in her seat. Then you revealed a specific challenge we face. The combination of all these elements made you appear strategic." Now you know the steps to replicate next time. Getting down to the behavioral level also enables you to adjust actions that aren't working so that you can avoid cementing bad habits.

- *Dig into compliments.* Your biggest learning opportunity will most likely come from an unexpected area: your strengths. Instead of what you did poorly and need to improve, useful feedback can also be based on what you already do well. How can you make your strength a superpower? For example, a leadership class participant once told me that he found me to be a passionate speaker. I asked, "What do I do or say that conveys passion, and what's the impact on you?" to which he replied, "You speak with your hands a lot and have large gestures. You also vary the tone of your voice quite a bit. The combination keeps me awake and inspires me to pay closer attention." Buoyed by his compliment, I was inspired to further study hand gestures and started using them more deliberately to land key points when speaking.

- *Listen to criticism—and be gracious.* If your manager does provide you with critical feedback, thank them. If their comments were confusing, paraphrase what you heard and verify that you understood them correctly. Ask short clarifying questions if necessary: "Would you please tell me more about point X?" "At which meeting did you notice this?" "How often have you seen me do this?" "Do you have an example?" Never explain away the feedback. Whether or not you agree with it, this is their perception of how you came across. You don't have to act on all the feedback you receive (in some cases, you might want to look into what someone shares before changing your behavior entirely), but if you want to keep receiving feedback, you have to act in a way that makes others want to give it to you.

After taking these steps, Tamara was finally able to get concrete feedback from her manager. By better understanding her manager's perception, she was able to operate at a more strategic level. She began developing her skills further and pointed out these changes to her boss—and she was promoted in the next performance review cycle.

. . .

To help you move up the promotion ladder, shed light on your blind spots and shine up your strengths. By taking charge of the process, you free up the feedback provider to do only one job: provide you with the input you need to become an outstanding executive.

Adapted from hbr.org, October 31, 2017. Reprint H03Z0N

4

Making Yourself Indispensable

by John H. Zenger, Joseph Folkman, and Scott K. Edinger

A manager we'll call Tom was a midlevel sales executive at a *Fortune* 500 company. After a dozen or so years there, he was thriving—he made his numbers, he was well liked, he got consistently positive reviews. He applied for a promotion that would put him in charge of a high-profile worldwide product-alignment initiative, confident that he was the top candidate and that this was the logical next move for him, a seemingly perfect fit for his skills and ambitions. His track record was solid. He'd made no stupid mistakes or career-limiting moves, and he'd had no run-ins with upper management. He was stunned, then, when a colleague with less experience got the job. What was the matter?

As far as Tom could tell, nothing. Everyone was happy with his work, his manager assured him, and a recent 360-degree assessment confirmed her view. Tom was at or above the norm in every area, strong not only in delivering results but also in problem solving, strategic thinking, and inspiring others to top performance. "No need to reinvent yourself," she said. "Just keep doing what you're doing. Go with your strengths."

But how? Tom was at a loss. Should he think more strategically? Become even more inspiring? Practice problem solving more intently?

It's pretty easy and straightforward to improve on a weakness; you can get steady, measurable results through linear development—that is, by learning and practicing basic techniques. But the data from our decades of work with tens of thousands of executives all over the world has shown us that developing strengths is very different. Doing more of what you already do well yields only incremental improvement. To get appreciably better at it, you have to work on complementary skills—what we call *nonlinear* development. This has long been familiar to athletes as cross-training. A novice runner, for example, benefits from doing stretching exercises and running a few times a week, gradually increasing mileage to build up endurance and muscle memory. But an experienced marathoner won't get significantly faster merely by running ever longer distances. To reach the next level, he needs to supplement that regimen by building up complementary skills through weight training, swimming, bicycling, interval training, yoga, and the like.

So it is with leadership competencies. To move from good to much better, you need to engage in the business equivalent of cross-training. If you're technically adept, for instance, delving even more deeply into technical manuals won't get you nearly as far as honing a complementary skill such as communication, which will make your expertise more apparent and accessible to your coworkers.

Idea in Brief

The Problem

Good leaders can become exceptional by developing just a few of their strengths to the highest level—but not by merely doing more of the same.

The Solution

Instead, they need to engage in the business equivalent of cross-training—that is, to enhance complementary skills that will enable them to make fuller use of their strengths.

For example, technical skills can become more effective when communication skills improve, making a leader's expertise more apparent and more accessible.

The Benefit

Once a few of their strengths have reached the level of outstanding, leaders become indispensable to their organizations despite the weaknesses they may have.

In this article we provide a simple guide to becoming a far more effective leader. We will see how Tom identified his strengths, decided which one to focus on and which complementary skill to develop, and what the results were. The process is straightforward, but complements are not always obvious. So first we'll take a closer look at the leadership equivalent of cross-training.

The Interaction Effect

In cross-training, the combination of two activities produces an improvement—an *interaction effect*—substantially greater than either one can produce on its own. There's nothing mysterious here. Combining diet with exercise, for example, has long been known to be substantially more effective in losing weight than either diet or exercise alone.

In our previous research we found 16 differentiating leadership competencies that correlate strongly with positive business outcomes such as increased profitability, employee engagement, revenue, and customer satisfaction. Among those 16, we wondered, could we find pairs that would produce significant interaction effects?

We searched through our database of more than a quarter million 360-degree surveys of some 30,000 developing leaders for pairings that resulted in far higher scores on overall leadership effectiveness than either attribute did on its own. The results were unambiguous. Take, for example, the competencies "focuses on results" and "builds relationships." Only 14% of leaders who were reasonably strong (that is, scored in the 75th percentile) in focusing on results but less so in building relationships reached the extraordinary leadership level: the 90th percentile in overall leadership effectiveness. Similarly, only 12% of those who were reasonably strong in building relationships but less so in focusing on results reached that level. But when an individual performed well in both categories, something dramatic happened: Fully 72% of those in the 75th percentile in both categories reached the 90th percentile in overall leadership effectiveness.

We measured the degree of correlation between overall leadership effectiveness and all possible pairings of our 16 differentiating competencies to learn which pairings were the most powerful. We also matched our 16 competencies with other leadership skills and measured how those pairs correlated with overall leadership effectiveness. We discovered that each of the 16 has up to a dozen associated behaviors—which we call *competency companions*—that were highly correlated with leadership excellence when combined with the differentiating competency.

(For a complete list of the competencies and their companions, see the exhibit "What skills will magnify my strengths?")

Consider the main competency "displays honesty and integrity." How would a leader go about improving a relative strength in this area? By being more honest? (We've heard that answer to the question many times.) That's not particularly useful advice. If an executive were weak in this area, we could recommend various ways to improve: Behave more consistently, avoid saying one thing and doing another, follow through on stated commitments, and so on. But a leader with high integrity is most likely already doing those things.

Our competency-companion research suggests a practical path forward. For example, assertiveness is among the behaviors that when paired with honesty and integrity correlate most strongly with high levels of overall leadership effectiveness. We don't mean to imply a causal relationship here: Assertiveness doesn't make someone honest, and integrity doesn't produce assertiveness. But if a highly principled leader learned to become more assertive, he might be more likely to speak up and act with the courage of his convictions, thus applying his strength more widely or frequently to become a more effective leader.

Our data suggest other ways in which a competency companion can reinforce a leadership strength. It might make the strength more apparent, as in the case of the technically strong leader who improves her ability to communicate. Or skills learned in developing the competency companion might be profitably applied to the main competency. A leader strong in innovativeness, for instance, might learn how to champion change, thus encouraging his team to achieve results in new and more creative ways.

What skills will magnify my strengths?

Our research shows that 16 leadership competencies correlate strongly with positive business outcomes. Each of them has up to a dozen "competency companions" whose development will strengthen the core skill.

Character

Displays honesty and integrity
- Shows concern and consideration for others
- Is trustworthy
- Demonstrates optimism
- Is assertive
- Inspires and motivates others
- Deals well with ambiguity
- Is decisive
- Focuses on results

Personal capability

Exhibits technical/professional expertise
- Solves problems and analyzes issues
- Builds relationships and networks
- Communicates powerfully and broadly
- Pursues excellence
- Takes initiative
- Develops others
- Displays honesty and integrity
- Acts in the team's best interest

Solves problems and analyzes issues
- Takes initiative
- Is organized and good at planning
- Is decisive
- Innovates
- Wants to tackle challenges
- Develops strategic perspective
- Acts independently
- Has technical expertise
- Communicates powerfully and broadly

Innovates
- Is willing to take risks and challenge the status quo
- Supports others in risk-taking
- Solves problems and analyzes issues
- Champions change
- Learns quickly from success and failure
- Develops strategic perspective
- Takes initiative

Practices self-development
- Listens
- Is open to others' ideas
- Respects others
- Displays honesty and integrity
- Inspires and motivates others
- Provides effective feedback and development
- Takes initiative
- Is willing to take risks and challenge the status quo

Getting results

Focuses on results
- Is organized and good at planning
- Displays honesty and integrity
- Anticipates problems
- Sees desired results clearly
- Provides effective feedback and development
- Establishes stretch goals
- Is personally accountable
- Is quick to act
- Provides rewards and recognition
- Creates a high-performance team
- Marshals adequate resources
- Innovates

Establishes stretch goals

- Inspires and motivates others
- Is willing to take risks and challenge the status quo
- Gains the support of others
- Develops strategic perspective
- Champions change
- Is decisive
- Has technical and business expertise
- Focuses on results

Takes initiative

- Anticipates problems
- Emphasizes speed
- Is organized and good at planning
- Champions others
- Deals well with ambiguity
- Follows through
- Inspires and motivates others
- Establishes stretch goals
- Displays honesty and integrity

Interpersonal skills

Communicates powerfully and broadly

- Inspires and motivates others
- Develops strategic perspective
- Establishes stretch goals
- Deals effectively with the outside world
- Is trustworthy
- Involves others
- Translates messages for clarity
- Solves problems and analyzes issues
- Takes initiative
- Innovates
- Develops others

Inspires and motivates others

- Connects emotionally with others
- Establishes stretch goals
- Exhibits clear vision and direction

- Communicates powerfully and broadly
- Develops others
- Collaborates and fosters teamwork
- Nurtures innovation
- Takes initiative
- Champions change
- Is a strong role model

Builds relationships

- Collaborates and fosters teamwork
- Displays honesty and integrity
- Develops others
- Listens
- Communicates powerfully and broadly
- Provides rewards and recognition
- Practices inclusion and values diversity
- Demonstrates optimism
- Practices self-development

Develops others

- Practices self-development
- Shows concern and consideration for others
- Is motivated by the success of others
- Practices inclusion and values diversity
- Develops strategic perspective
- Provides effective feedback and development
- Inspires and motivates others
- Innovates
- Provides rewards and recognition
- Displays honesty and integrity

Collaborates and fosters teamwork

- Is trustworthy
- Builds relationships and networks
- Practices inclusion and values diversity
- Develops strategic perspective

(continued)

What skills will magnify my strengths? (*continued*)

Collaborates and fosters teamwork
(*continued*)
- Establishes stretch goals
- Communicates powerfully and broadly
- Displays honesty and integrity
- Adapts to change
- Inspires and motivates others
- Develops others

Leading change
Develops strategic perspective
- Focuses on customers
- Innovates
- Solves problems and analyzes issues
- Communicates powerfully and broadly
- Establishes stretch goals
- Demonstrates business acumen
- Champions change
- Inspires and motivates others

Champions change
- Inspires and motivates others

- Builds relationships and networks
- Develops others
- Provides rewards and recognition
- Practices inclusion and values
  diversity
- Innovates
- Focuses on results
- Is willing to take risks and challenge
  the status quo
- Develops strategic perspective

Connects the group to the
outside world
- Develops broad perspective
- Develops strategic perspective
- Inspires and motivates others
- Has strong interpersonal skills
- Takes initiative
- Gathers and assimilates information
- Champions change
- Communicates powerfully and
  broadly

Building Strengths, Step by Step

As a practical matter, cross-training for leadership skills is clear-cut: (1) Identify your strengths. (2) Choose a strength to focus on according to its importance to the organization and how passionately you feel about it. (3) Select a complementary behavior you'd like to enhance. (4) Develop it in a linear way.

Identify your strengths

Strengths can arguably be identified in a variety of ways. But we contend that in the context of effective leadership, your view of your own (or even some perfectly objective view, supposing one could be had) is less important than other people's, because leadership is all about your effect on others. That's why we start with a 360—as Tom did.

Ideally, you should go about this in a psychometrically valid way, through a formal process in which you and your direct reports, peers, and bosses anonymously complete questionnaires ranking your leadership attributes on a quantitative scale. You and they should also answer some qualitative, open-ended questions concerning your strengths, your fatal flaws (if any), and the relative importance of those attributes to the company. By "fatal flaws," we mean flaws so critical that they can overpower any strengths you have or may develop—flaws that can derail your career.

Not every organization is able or willing to conduct 360s for everyone. So if that's not feasible, you may be able to solicit qualitative data from your colleagues if—and this is a big caveat— you can make them feel comfortable enough to be honest in their feedback. You could create your own feedback form and ask people to return it anonymously. (See the sidebar "An Informal 360" for a suggested set of questions.) We have also seen earnest one-on-one conversations work for this purpose; if nothing else, they show your coworkers that you are genuinely interested in self-improvement. (Nevertheless, it's unlikely that anyone will tell you directly if you have fatal flaws.)

In interpreting the results, people commonly focus first on their lowest scores. But unless those are extremely low (in the 10th percentile), that's a mistake. (We have found that 20% of executives do typically discover such a critical problem in their 360s; if you're among them, you must fix the flaw, which you can do in a linear way.)

An Informal 360

Before you can build on your strengths, you need an objective view of what they are. Ideally, this comes from a formal, confidential 360-degree evaluation. But if that's not possible, a direct approach can work. Try simply asking your team members, colleagues, and boss these simple questions, either in person or in writing.

- What leadership skills do you think are strengths for me?

- Is there anything I do that might be considered a fatal flaw— that could derail my career or lead me to fail in my current job if it's not addressed?

- What leadership ability, if outstanding, would have the most significant impact on the productivity or effectiveness of the organization?

- What leadership abilities of mine have the most significant impact on you?

Do your best to exhibit receptiveness and to create a feeling of safety (especially for direct reports). Make it clear that you're seeking self-improvement. Tell your colleagues explicitly that you are open to negative feedback and that you will absorb it professionally and appropriately—and without retribution. Of course, you need to follow through on this promise, or the entire process will fail.

What makes leaders indispensable to their organizations, our data unmistakably show, is not being good at many things but being uniquely outstanding at a few things. Such strengths allow a leader's inevitable weaknesses to be overlooked. The executives in our database who exhibited no profound (that is, in the 90th percentile) strengths scored only in the 34th percentile, on average, in overall leadership effectiveness. But if they had just one outstanding strength, their overall leadership effectiveness score rose to the 64th percentile, on average. In other words, the difference between being in the bottom third of leaders and being almost in the top third is a single extraordinary strength. Two profound strengths put leaders close to the top quartile, three put them in the top quintile, and four put them nearly in the top decile. (See the exhibit "What difference can a single strength make?")

In this context, a look at Tom's 360 results sheds light on the question of why he was passed over for a plum assignment. Tom had no critical flaws, but he hadn't yet demonstrated any outstanding strengths either. With no strengths above the 70th percentile, he didn't score "good," let alone "outstanding," in overall leadership ability. Anyone in the organization with a single notable strength was likely to outpace him for promotion opportunities. But if Tom could lift just a few of his relative strengths from the 70th to the 80th and then the 90th percentile, his overall leadership effectiveness might go from above average to good to exceptional. Clearly, those strengths merited a closer examination.

Like many people, though, Tom was initially galvanized by the low bars on his chart, which evoked a mixture of guilt and denial. His relatively low score on building relationships called up uncomfortable memories of high school—something he didn't mention as he looked over the results with his boss. But he did say that he couldn't believe he wasn't scored higher on innovativeness, and he started to tick off initiatives he felt he deserved credit for. Maybe he was innovative, and maybe he wasn't. It's common for your self-assessment to vary sharply from everyone else's assessment of you. But remember that it's others' opinions that matter.

What difference can a single strength make?

Raising just one competency to the level of outstanding can up your overall leadership effectiveness ranking from the bottom third to almost the top third.

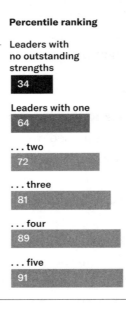

Percentile ranking

Leaders with
no outstanding
strengths
34

Leaders with one
64

... two
72

... three
81

... four
89

... five
91

When Tom did turn his attention to his strengths, he wasn't surprised to see that he scored well in focusing on results and in solving problems and analyzing issues. Less obvious to him, and perhaps more gratifying, were his relatively high marks in developing strategic perspective and inspiring and motivating others. Now he could move on to the next step.

Choose a strength to focus on

Choices between good and bad are easy. But choices between good and good cause us to deliberate and second-guess. It may not matter which competency Tom selected, since enhancing any one of them would markedly improve his leadership effectiveness.

Nevertheless, we recommend that developing leaders focus on a competency that matters to the organization and about which they feel some passion, because a strength you feel passionate about that is not important to your organization is essentially a hobby, and a strength the organization needs that you don't feel passionate about is just a chore.

You can use your colleagues' importance ratings from the 360 assessment to get a somewhat objective view of organizational needs. But the prospect of following his passions alarmed Tom, who didn't know how to begin. Answering a series of questions made the notion more concrete. For each of the 16 competencies, he ran down the following list:

- Do I look for ways to enhance this skill?

- Do I look for new ways to use it?

- Am I energized, not exhausted, when I use it?

- Do I pursue projects in which I can apply this strength?

- Can I imagine devoting time to improving it?

- Would I enjoy getting better at this skill?

Counting his "yes" answers gave Tom a solid way to quantify his passions. A simple worksheet showed him how his skills, his passions, and the organization's needs dovetailed (see the exhibit "Narrowing down the options"). When Tom checked off his top five competencies, his five passions, and the organization's top priorities, he could see a clear convergence. He decided to focus on the strength that, as it happens, we have found to be most universally associated with extraordinary leadership: "inspires and motivates others."

Narrowing down the options

The strength you focus on should be both important to the organization and important to you. A simple worksheet (like Tom's, below) can help you see where your strengths and interests and the needs of your organization converge. Choose five competencies in each of the three categories.

	Your competencies	Your passions	Organizational needs	Total
1. Displays honesty and integrity				
2. Exhibits technical/professional expertise	X			1
3. Solves problems and analyzes issues	X			1
4. Innovates		X	X	2
5. Practices self-development				
6. Focuses on results	X			1
7. Establishes stretch goals				
8. Takes initiative		X		1
9. Communicates powerfully and broadly			X	1
10. Inspires and motivates others	X	X	X	③
11. Builds relationships			X	1
12. Develops others		X		1
13. Collaborates and fosters teamwork		X		1
14. Develops strategic perspective	X		X	2
15. Champions change				
16. Connects the group to the outside world				

Select a complementary behavior

People who excel at motivating others are good at persuading them to take action and to go the extra mile. They effectively exercise power to influence key decisions for the benefit of the organization. They know how to motivate different people in different ways. So it was not surprising that Tom already did those things pretty well. He scanned the list of competency companions:

- Connects emotionally with others

- Establishes stretch goals

- Exhibits clear vision and direction

- Communicates powerfully and broadly

- Develops others

- Collaborates and fosters teamwork

- Nurtures innovation

- Takes initiative

- Champions change

- Is a strong role model

You should choose a companion behavior that, like a good strength, is important to the organization and makes you feel enthusiastic about tackling it. But at this point it's also constructive to consider your lower scores. In talking these points over with his manager, Tom decided to work on his communication skills, which didn't score particularly high but were high enough that raising them a little could make a significant difference.

Develop it in a linear way

Having settled on a competency companion, Tom could now work at directly improving his basic skills in that area. Strong communicators speak concisely and deliver effective presentations.

Their instructions are clear. They write well. They can explain new concepts clearly. They help people understand how their work contributes to broader business objectives. They can translate terms used by people in different functions. Tom saw lots of room for improvement here: No one would ever call him concise; he didn't always finish sentences he'd started; and he found writing a challenge.

We would have recommended that he look for as many opportunities as possible, both inside and outside work, to improve his communication. He could take a course in business writing. He could practice with friends and family, in his church or his community. He could volunteer to make presentations to senior management or ask colleagues to critique some of his memos and emails. He might volunteer to help high school students write college application essays. He could videotape himself making speeches or join a local Toastmasters club.

Tom decided to seek the advice of a colleague whose communication skills he admired. The colleague suggested (among other things) that because writing was not a strong point, Tom should practice communicating more in person or over the phone. This turned out to be challenging: Tom found that before he could even begin, he had to change his approach to email, because he was in the habit of constantly checking and replying to it throughout the day. He couldn't always substitute the phone, because he couldn't make calls while he was in a meeting or talking to someone else. He started to set aside specific times of the day for email so that he could reply by phone or in person—a small change that had unexpected consequences. Instead of being interrupted and distracted at random moments throughout the day (and evening), his staffers had concentrated, direct interactions with him. They found these more efficient and effective, even though they could no longer choose when (or whether) to reply to Tom's cryptic emails. Tom found that he connected better with people he talked to, both because his attention wasn't divided between them and his BlackBerry and because he could read their tone of voice and body language. As a result, he absorbed more information, and his colleagues felt he was more attentive to their views.

Tom also started to pay more attention not just to how he was communicating but to what he was saying. His colleague suggested that Tom start to keep track of how often he issued instructions versus how often he asked questions. Tom also took note of how much of what he said was criticism (constructive or otherwise) and how much was encouragement. Increasing the proportion of questions and encouragement had an immediate effect: His team began to understand him more quickly, so he didn't have to repeat himself as often. Several team members actually thanked him for allowing them to express their points of view.

Like Tom, you should expect to see some concrete evidence of improvement within 30 to 60 days. If you don't, what you're doing is not working. That said, complementary behaviors improve steadily with practice, and Tom's progress is typical: Fifteen months later, on taking another 360, he found he'd moved into the 82nd percentile in his ability to inspire. He wasn't extraordinary yet, but he was getting close. Our advice would be to keep at it—to improve another competency companion or two until he reaches the 90th percentile and becomes truly exceptional at inspiring others. Then he can start the entire process again with another strength and its complements, and another—at which point he will be making a uniquely valuable contribution to his company.

Can You Overdo It?

Everyone knows someone who is too assertive, too technically oriented, too focused on driving for results. Many people cite examples like these to argue against the wisdom of improving your leadership effectiveness by strengthening your strengths. Our research does in fact show a point where balance becomes important. The data suggest that the difference between having four profound strengths and having five is a gain of merely 2 percentage points in overall leadership effectiveness. Thus leaders who are already exceptional should consider one more variable.

You will note in the exhibit "What skills will magnify my strengths?" that the 16 differentiating competencies fall into five broader categories: character, personal capability, getting results, interpersonal skills, and leading change. People who have many strengths should consider how they are distributed across those categories and focus improvement efforts on an underrepresented one.

But we cannot think of a less constructive approach to improving your leadership effectiveness than treating your strengths as weaknesses. Have you ever known anyone who had too much integrity? Was too effective a communicator? Was just too inspiring? Developing competency companions works precisely because, rather than simply doing more of the same, you are enhancing how you already behave with new ways of working and interacting that will make that behavior more effective.

. . .

Focusing on your strengths is hardly a new idea. Forty-four years ago Peter Drucker made the business case eloquently in *The*

Effective Executive: "Unless . . . an executive looks for strength and works at making strength productive, he will only get the impact of what a man cannot do, of his lacks, his weaknesses, his impediments to performance and effectiveness. To staff from what there is not and to focus on weakness is wasteful—a misuse, if not abuse, of the human resource." Since then a body of work has grown up supporting and advocating for Drucker's approach. Our own research shows how big a difference developing a few strengths can make. It is distressing to find that fewer than 10% of the executives we work with have any plan to do so.

We are convinced that the problem is less a matter of conviction than of execution. Executives need a path to enhancing their strengths that is as clear as the one to fixing their weaknesses. That is the greatest value, we believe, of the cross-training approach: It allows people to use the linear improvement techniques they know and understand to produce a nonlinear result.

Often executives complain to us that there are not enough good leaders in their organizations. We would argue that in fact far too many leaders are merely good. The challenge is not to replace bad leaders with good ones; it is to turn people like Tom—hardworking, capable executives who are reasonably good at their jobs—into outstanding leaders with distinctive strengths.

Originally published in October 2011. Reprint R1110E

5

The Art of Asking Smarter Questions

by Arnaud Chevallier, Frédéric Dalsace, and Jean-Louis Barsoux

A s a cofounder and the CEO of the U.S. chipmaker Nvidia, Jensen Huang operates in a high-velocity industry requiring agile, innovative thinking. Reflecting on how his leadership style has evolved, he told the *New York Times*, "I probably give fewer answers and I ask a lot more questions. . . . It's almost possible now for me to go through a day and do nothing but ask questions." He continued, "Through probing, I help [my management team] . . . explore ideas that they didn't realize needed to be explored."

The urgency and unpredictability long faced by tech companies have spread to more-mature sectors, elevating inquiry as an essential skill. Advances in AI have caused a seismic shift from a world in which answers were crucial to one in which questions are. The big differentiator is no longer access to information but the ability to craft smart prompts. "As a leader, you don't have the answers; your workforce [does], your people [do]," Jane Fraser, Citi's CEO, told *Fortune* magazine. "That's completely changed how you have to lead an organization. You have to unleash the creativity. . . . The innovation isn't happening because there's a genius at the top of the company that's coming up with the answers for everything."

Indeed, leaders have embraced the importance of listening, curiosity, learning, and humility—qualities critical to skillful interrogation. "Question-storming"—brainstorming for questions rather than answers—is now a creativity technique. But unlike lawyers, doctors, and psychologists, business leaders aren't formally trained on what kinds of questions to ask. They must learn as they go.

It's not a matter of asking lots of questions in hopes of eventually hitting on the right ones. Corinne Dauger, a former VP of creative development at Hermès, told us, "In a one-hour meeting, there are only so many questions you can ask. . . . So where do you want to spend the time? When you're asking one question, you're not asking another." If any one line of questioning dominates, it inevitably crowds out others. Leaders must also watch for complacency, diminishing returns, avoidance of sensitive topics, and stubbornness.

In our research and consulting over the past decade, we've seen that certain kinds of questions have gained resonance across the business world. And in a three-year project we asked executives to question-storm about the decisions they've faced and the kinds of inquiry they've pursued. In this article we share what we've learned. We offer a practical framework for the types of questions to ask in strategic decision-making and a tool to help you assess your interrogatory style.

Idea in Brief

The Situation

With organizations of all sorts facing increased urgency and uncertainty, the ability to ask smart questions has become key. But, *most people* aren't formally trained in that skill.

Why It's So Challenging

Managers' expertise often blinds them to new ideas. And the flow of questions can be hard to process in real time, so certain concerns and insights may never be raised.

The Remedy

Strategic questions can be grouped into five domains: investigative, speculative, productive, interpretive, and subjective. By attending to each, leaders and teams are more likely to cover all the areas that need to be explored—and they'll surface information and options they might otherwise have missed.

The Great Unasked Questions

Before we lay out our framework, we want to emphasize one point above all: The questions that get leaders and teams into trouble are often the ones they fail to ask. These are questions that don't come spontaneously; they require prompting and conscious effort. They may run counter to your and your team's individual or collective habits, preoccupations, and patterns of interaction.

The late scholar and business thinker Sumantra Ghoshal once said that leadership means making happen what otherwise would not. In the realm of inquiry a leader's job is to flush out information, insights, and alternatives, unearthing critical questions the team has overlooked. You don't need to come up with the missing questions yourself, but you do need to draw attention to neglected spheres of inquiry so that others can raise them.

All this is harder than it may sound, for two reasons. First, you may be hampered by your expertise. Your professional successes and deep experience may have skewed your approach to problem-solving. It can be hard to escape the gravitational pull of such conditioning unless you take a hard look at your question habits. Second, the flow and diversity of questions can be hard to process in real time, especially amid heated exchanges. Often it's only after the fact that you realize certain concerns or options were never raised.

Our research reveals that strategic questions can be grouped into five domains: *investigative, speculative, productive, interpretive,* and *subjective.* Each unlocks a different aspect of the decision-making process. Together they can help you tackle key issues that are all too easy to miss.

Investigative: What's known?

When they are facing a problem or an opportunity, effective decision-makers start by clarifying their purpose—asking themselves what they want to achieve and what they need to learn to do so. The process can be fueled by using successive "Why?" questions, as in the "five whys" sequence devised by managers at Toyota. Successively asking "How?" can also help you transcend generic solutions and develop more-sophisticated alternatives. Investigative questions dig ever deeper to generate nonobvious information. The most common mistake is failing to go deep enough.

It sounds like a straightforward process, but lapses are surprisingly common. In 2014 a failure of investigation led a team at the French rail operator SNCF to neglect an essential piece of data during its €15 billion purchase of 1,860 regional trains. No one thought to ask whether the platform measurements were universal. They weren't. The trains proved too wide for 1,300 older stations—a mistake that cost €50 million to fix. The Spanish train operator Renfe discovered a similar oversight in 2021: The 31 state-of-the-art commuter trains it had ordered were too big to pass through some tunnels in the mountainous areas they were meant to serve. The problem was detected before the trains were built, but delivery was significantly delayed.

Speculative: What if?

Whereas investigative questions help you identify and analyze a problem in depth, speculative questions help you consider it more broadly. To reframe the problem or explore more-creative solutions, leaders must ask things like "What if . . . ?" and "What else . . . ?" The global design company IDEO popularized this approach. It systematically uses the prompt "How might we . . . ?"—coined by Min Basadur when he was a young manager at P&G—to overcome limiting assumptions and jump-start creative problem-solving.

Consider how Emirates Team New Zealand's innovative catamaran won international sport's oldest extant trophy, the America's Cup, in 2017. Crew members pedaled stationary bikes to generate power for the vessel's hydraulic systems rather than turning handles, as was customary. Many observers assumed that the breakthrough question had been "What if we used leg power instead of arm power?" That wasn't a new suggestion, however. Other competitors had considered and rejected the idea, unwilling to hamper crew members' ability to move around the boat. One team had even tried it.

The team from New Zealand went a step further, asking, "What else could a pedal system allow?" It could free up crew members' hands, the team realized, and the boat's hydraulic systems could then be operated with handlebar controls. That distributed the crew's roles more evenly and allowed multiple maneuvers to be executed quickly. The boat could be sailed more precisely and aggressively, leading to an upset win over Oracle Team USA.

Productive: Now what?

Productive questions help you assess the availability of talent, capabilities, time, and other resources. They influence the speed of decision-making, the introduction of initiatives, and the pace of growth.

In the 1990s the CEO of AlliedSignal, Larry Bossidy, famously integrated a focus on execution into his company's culture. He insisted on rigorously questioning and rethinking the various hows of executing on strategy: "How can we get it done?" "How will we synchronize our actions?" "How will we measure progress?" and so on. Such questions can help you identify key metrics and milestones—along with possible bottlenecks—to align your people and projects and keep your plans on track. They will expose risks, including strains on the organization's capacity.

The top team at Lego neglected productive questions when responding to the rise of digital toys in the early 2000s. The toymaker tried to diversify its way out of trouble, introducing several products in rapid succession. The initiatives themselves weren't necessarily misguided, but each meant a stretch into an adjacent area, such as software (Lego Movie Maker), learning concepts (Lego Education), or clothing (Lego Wear). Collectively they far exceeded the company's bandwidth, and Lego suffered record losses in 2003. The following year the incoming CEO, Jørgen Vig Knudstorp, shared his diagnosis of the problem with the board: "Rather than doing one adjacency every three to five years, we did three to five adjacencies every year." He later told the MIT professor David Robertson, "Suddenly we had to manage a lot of businesses that we just didn't understand. We didn't have the capabilities, and we couldn't keep up the pace."

Interpretive: So, what . . . ?

Interpretive questions—sensemaking questions—enable synthesis. They push you to continually redefine the core issue—to go beneath the surface and ask, "What is this problem really about?" Natural follow-ups to investigative, speculative, and productive questions, interpretive questions draw out the implications of an observation or an idea. After an investigative question, you might ask, "So, what happens if this trend continues?" After a speculative question, "So, what opportunities does that idea open up?" After a productive question, "So, what does that imply for scaling up or sequencing?"

Interpretive questions come in other forms, too: "What did we learn from this?" "How is that useful?" "Are these the right questions to ask?" In an interview on *The Tim Ferriss Show*, Daniel Ek reflected on what he considered his chief role as the CEO of Spotify: "It's almost always back to purpose—like, Why are we doing things? Why does it matter? How does this ladder up to the mission?"

A decision-making process should always circle back to interpretive questions. They provide the momentum to move from one mode of inquiry to another, and they convert information into actionable insight. Even solid analyses are ineffectual if you fail to make sense of them. Ten years ago we worked with the top team at a high-end European car manufacturer. When we brought up Tesla's recently released all-electric sedan, some of the engineers laughed. "There's a seven-millimeter gap between the door and the chassis," one said. "These people don't know how to make a car."

That was a serious error of sensemaking. By focusing on a technical imperfection, the automaker failed to spot the car's revolutionary appeal and missed the urgent competitive questions it should have raised.

Subjective: What's unsaid?

The final category of questions differs from all the others. Whereas they deal with the substance of a challenge, it deals with the personal reservations, frustrations, tensions, and hidden agendas that can push decision-making off course. Volocopter's CEO, Dirk Hoke, once told us, "When we fail, it's often because we haven't considered the emotional part."

The notion of people issues as a competitive advantage gained prominence in the aviation industry in the early 1980s. Herb Kelleher, then the CEO of Southwest Airlines, recognized that the customer experience could be dramatically improved by putting employees first and empowering them to treat people right. SAS's CEO, Jan Carlzon, transformed the Scandinavian airline by "inverting the pyramid" to support customer-facing staffers in "moments of truth." In both cases the role of managers became to coach and support—not monitor and control—frontline staff. They learned to ask their *internal* customers, "How can I help?"

If you neglect this mode of questioning or fail to push hard enough in it, your proposed solution might be undone by subjective reactions even though your analysis, insights, and plans are sound. British Airways is a cautionary example. In 1997 it was the world's leading carrier of international passengers, but surveys showed that it was viewed as staid and stuffy. So CEO Robert Ayling and his team decided to boost the airline's global image by replacing the British colors on the planes' tail fins with ethnic designs by artists from around the world.

The designs were visually striking, but the top team badly misgauged employees' and customers' emotional reactions. The staff was distressed that a £60 million rebrand had been undertaken amid ongoing cost-saving measures. British business travelers—the airline's core customers—were strongly attached to the national branding and antagonized by its removal. And as if to underline the error, Virgin CEO Richard Branson announced that his planes would proudly "fly the flag." BA's new designs were withdrawn two years later, and the misjudgment contributed to Ayling's ouster.

Team members may be reluctant to explore emotional issues unless the leader provides encouragement and a safe space for discussion. They may fail to share misgivings simply because no one else is doing so—a social dynamic known as *pluralistic ignorance*. Leaders must invite dissenting views and encourage doubters to share their concerns.

Balancing Your Question Mix

We created a tool to help people assess their questioning styles and gave it to 1,200 global executives. Although the combined results showed an even distribution among the five styles we've described, individual answers revealed major imbalances. One category or another was barely on the radar of more than a third of the executives. And follow-up interviews showed that many leaders were overly attached to the types of questions that had

What's Your Question Mix?

The questions below are taken from the self-assessment we use with executives and their teams. Our wording here is very direct to avoid ambiguity, but you'll want to be more diplomatic in practice. Reflect on the five sets of questions and think about which ones come most naturally to you and which feel less comfortable, rating them on a scale of 1 (not part of my repertoire) to 5 (one of my go-tos). Compare the totals for each section and focus your attention on the lowest-scoring sets.

Investigative

- What happened?
- What is and isn't working?
- What are the causes of the problem?
- How feasible and desirable is each option?
- What evidence supports our proposed plan?

Speculative

- What other scenarios might exist?
- Could we do this differently?
- What else might we propose?
- What can we simplify, combine, modify, reverse, or eliminate?
- What potential solutions have we not considered?

brought them success. They relied on those at the expense of other kinds of inquiries.

Assess your current question style

Self-awareness is an essential first step, of course, toward correcting or compensating for weaknesses. For insight into your

Productive

- What is the next step?

- What do we need to achieve before taking it?

- Do we have the resources to move ahead?

- Do we know enough to proceed?

- Are we ready to decide?

Interpretive

- What did we learn from this new information?

- What does it mean for our present and future actions?

- What should be our overarching goal?

- How does this fit with that goal?

- What are we trying to achieve?

Subjective

- How do you really feel about this decision?

- Are there differences between what was said, what was heard, and what was meant?

- Have we consulted the right people?

- Are all stakeholders genuinely aligned?

questioning preferences and habits, you can take an abridged version of our self-assessment. After you've identified your strong points and weaknesses, three tactics can improve your mix. You can adjust your repertoire of questions; change your emphasis to reflect evolving needs; and surround yourself with people who compensate for your blind spots.

Adjust your repertoire

Having established which types of questions you are most and least comfortable asking, you need to create a better balance. One way to begin is to remind yourself of the five categories before your next decision-making meeting and ensure that you're considering all of them. The CHRO at a large tech company we worked with had us display the framework throughout an important company program.

You can also try out questions from your weak or missing categories in a few low-stakes situations. That will help you understand how things you're not accustomed to asking can open up a discussion. Steven Baert, a former chief people and organization officer at Novartis, described his process on *The Curious Advantage* podcast. "Previously [I focused on] listening to fix," he told the host. "'You have a problem. I need a few points of data from you so I can solve the problem.' [But now] I'm practicing listening to learn."

There's another step involved in adjusting your repertoire: You may need to discard some types of questions that served you well in the past. This point was captured in a *Financial Times* profile of Erick Brimen, CEO of the investment group NeWay Capital, who describes himself as a stubborn, goal-oriented micromanager. "The lesson I've been learning," he said, "is to let go of the 'how to get there' and to focus on 'where we are going.'"

Change your emphasis

Your question mix is a moving target, especially if you're now in a new role, company, or industry. As you take on bigger responsibilities, for instance, you'll face increasingly complex challenges, not just because they have more components but also because you're allowed to take larger leaps. Reflecting on her own trajectory, Patricia Corsi, the chief marketing, digital, and information officer at Bayer Consumer Health, told us, "As your career progresses, you're offered riskier moves, into jobs you've never done, domains you don't know, and challenges you've never experienced. . . . [People] gamble on your ability to ask the questions that will help you learn."

With every job change, you face a challenge to adapt. The question mix that previously worked for you and helped you land your new role might now lead you astray. We spoke with Larry Dominique when he was adjusting to his new position as the SVP and head of Alfa Romeo and Fiat North America. "Drawing on my experience as an engineer, I'll go deeper into costs, resources-management efficiency, and customer satisfaction," he told us. But he recognized the danger of playing only to his established strengths: "I have to remind myself that my real value as a leader is to provide the big picture and to move beyond the questions that are comfortable for me."

Find others who can compensate

As previously noted, you don't need to come up with all the questions yourself; it should be a team effort. José Muñoz, the global president and COO of Hyundai Motor Company, sometimes delegates the questioner role. "The person who asks the question should be the one who's best equipped," he told us. "As the boss, I might invite someone on my team to continue a line of questioning." After completing his self-assessment, Robert Jasiński, then the managing director of Danone in Romania, said, "I'll pay more attention to what I value the least [the speculative category]. And if someone on my team is a good creative thinker, I'll do a better job of listening to what they have to say."

As a leader, you're responsible for noticing missing perspectives and giving people a chance to contribute. Gilles Morel, the president of Whirlpool Europe, Middle East, and Africa, told us, "I need to make space for the people who aren't like me to ask these questions that I'm not good at asking." But getting everyone to contribute may not be easy. A change of leadership style to a more inquisitive approach can feel threatening. And the same query may elicit either vital input or defensiveness, depending on how it's phrased. One HR specialist finds that "Why?" questions sometimes trigger resistance and that a simple change to "How come . . . ?" gets better results. David Loew, CEO of the biopharmaceutical company Ipsen, told us, "If you start asking closed or loaded questions, such as 'Why have you done it like this?,' it can feel like a police interrogation. That creates an unsafe space, and unease spreads to the rest of the team."

At least as important as the words used are the perceived attitude and intention of the questioner. The question "Is everyone OK with that?," for example, can be heard as either a genuine invitation to share reservations or an attempt to shut down the discussion. "When I ask searching questions, I make it clear that it's OK if you don't have an answer, or if you don't have one right away," Charles Bouaziz, CEO of the medical technology group MTD, told us. "Your tone often matters more than the question. People sometimes assume you're testing them." Problems of interpretation are exacerbated in virtual meetings, where intention is harder to assess; you can't be sure how your question has landed. "Without the full body cues of in-person meetings, leaders have to lean even more strongly into asking the right questions, and listening for misunderstandings or trigger points," Lisa Curtis, the founder and CEO of Kuli Kuli Foods, wrote in *Inc.* magazine.

You'll need to educate your team about the various kinds of questions and the importance of attending to all of them. Some of the most successful executives we know always start conversations with new people by creating a safe space and demonstrating openness and vulnerability. They operate in what Marilee Adams, the author of *Change Your Questions, Change Your Life* and the founder of the Inquiry Institute, calls "learner mode," as opposed to "judger mode." The former is expansive and focuses on assumptions, possibilities, solutions, and meaningful action. The latter is reactive and shortsighted and focuses on discovering who's to blame.

But even when the entire team contributes, there's no guarantee that all five kinds of questions will be covered, especially in high-stress situations. Team members may have a shared blind spot. If that's the case, try assigning one question type to each member—at least until the group's collective repertoire is reasonably well balanced.

To Gilles Morel, the end goal is clear. "I want to create a questioning muscle within the team," he has said. "I need to set the stage so that my curiosity is amplified by the curiosity of others. Their questions should stimulate my questions." His remarks echo Jensen Huang's belief that leadership involves "getting everybody to ask and answer questions."

. . .

By pinpointing the strengths and weaknesses in your interrogatory styles and considering the five types of questions we've outlined, you and your team can make smarter strategic deci-sions. You'll be more likely to cover all the critical areas that need to be explored—and you'll surface information, insights, and options you might otherwise have missed.

Originally published in May–June 2024. Reprint R2403C

6

A Smarter Way to Network

**by Rob Cross and
Robert J. Thomas**

One of the happiest, most successful executives we know is a woman named Deb. She works at a major technology company and runs a global business unit that has more than 7,000 employees. When you ask her how she rose to the top and why she enjoys her job, her answer is simple: people. She points to her boss, the CEO, a mentor who "always has her back"; Steve, the head of a complementary business, with whom she has monthly brainstorming lunches and occasional gripe sessions; and Tom, a protégé to whom she has delegated responsibility for a large portion of her division. Outside the company, Deb's circle includes her counterparts in three strategic partnerships, who inspire her with new ideas; Sheila, a former colleague, now in a different industry, who gives her candid feedback; and her husband, Bob, an executive at a philanthropic organization. She also has close relationships with her fellow volunteers in a program for at-risk high school students and the members of her tennis group and book club.

This is Deb's social network (the real-world kind, not the virtual kind), and it has helped her career a lot. But not because the group is large or full of high-powered contacts. Her network is effective because it both supports and challenges her. Deb's relationships help her gain influence, broaden her expertise, learn new skills, and find purpose and balance. Deb values and nurtures them. "Make friends so that you have friends when you need friends" is her motto.

"My current role is really a product of a relationship I formed over a decade ago that came back to me at the right time," she explains. "People may chalk it up to luck, but I think more often than not luck happens through networks where people give first and are authentic in all they do."

Over the past 15 years, we've worked with many executives like Deb, at more than 300 companies. What began as organizational research—helping management teams understand and capitalize on the formal and informal social networks of their employees—has since metamorphosed into personal programs, which teach individual executives to increase their effectiveness by leveraging their networks.

The old adage "It's not what you know, it's who you know" is true. But it's more nuanced than that. In spite of what most self-help books say, network size doesn't usually matter. In fact, we've found that individuals who simply know a lot of people are less likely to achieve standout performance, because they're spread too thin. Political animals with lots of connections to

Idea in Brief

The Problem

The adage "It's not what you know, it's who you know" is true. The right social network can have a huge impact on your success. But many people misunderstand what makes a network strong: They believe the key is maintaining a large circle filled with high-powered contacts. That's not the right approach.

The Opportunity

The networks of the happiest highest-performing executives are different: They're select but diverse, made up of high-quality relationships with people who come from varying spheres and from up and down the corporate ladder. They help managers learn, make decisions with less bias, and grow personally.

The Solution

The most effective networks include six critical kinds of connections: people who provide information, ideas, or expertise; formally and informally powerful people, who offer mentoring and political support; people who give developmental feedback; people who lend personal support; people who increase your sense of purpose or worth; and people who promote work-life balance. If your network doesn't look like this, you can follow a four-step process to improve it. You'll need to identify who your connections are and what they offer you, back away from redundant and energy-draining connections, fill holes in your network with the right kind of people, and work to make the most of your contacts. Do this, and in due course, you'll have a network that steers the best opportunities, ideas, and talent your way.

corporate and industry leaders don't win the day, either. Yes, it's important to know powerful people, but if they account for too much of your network, your peers and subordinates often perceive you to be overly self-interested, and you may lose support as a result.

The data we've collected point to a different model for networking. The executives who consistently rank in the top 20% of their companies in both performance and well-being have diverse but select networks like Deb's—made up of high-quality relationships with people who come from several different spheres and from up and down the corporate hierarchy. These high performers, we have found, tap into six critical kinds of connections, which enhance their careers and lives in a variety of ways.

Through our work advising individual managers, we've also identified a four-step process that will help any executive develop this kind of network. But first, let's take a look at some common networking mistakes.

Getting It Wrong

Many people take a misguided approach to networking. They go astray by building imbalanced networks, pursuing the wrong kind of relationships, or leveraging relationships ineffectively. (See the sidebar "Are You Networking Impaired?") These people might remain successful for a time, but often they will hit a plateau or see their career derailed because their networks couldn't prompt or support a critical transition.

Consider Dan, the chief information officer of one of the world's largest life sciences organizations. He was under constant pressure to find new technologies that would spur innovation and speed the drug commercialization process at his company, and he needed a network that would help him. Unfortunately, more than 70% of his trusted advisers were in the unit he had worked in before becoming CIO. Not only did they

Are You Networking Impaired?

In our work, we have identified six common managerial types who get stuck in three kinds of network traps. Do any of the descriptions below fit you?

The Wrong Structure

The formalist focuses too heavily on his company's official hierarchy, missing out on the efficiencies and opportunities that come from informal connections.

The overloaded manager has so much contact with colleagues and external ties that she becomes a bottleneck to progress and burns herself out.

The Wrong Relationships

The disconnected expert sticks with people who keep him focused on safe, existing competencies, rather than those who push him to build new skills.

The biased leader relies on advisers much like herself (same functional background, location, or values), who reinforce her biases, when she should instead seek outsiders to prompt more fully informed decisions.

The Wrong Behavior

The superficial networker engages in surface-level interaction with as many people as possible, mistakenly believing that a bigger network is a better one.

The chameleon changes his interests, values, and personality to match those of whatever subgroup is his audience, and winds up being disconnected from every group.

reinforce his bias toward certain solutions and vendors, but they lacked the outside knowledge he needed. "I had started to mistake friendship, trust, and accessibility for real expertise in new domains," he told us. "This didn't mean I was going to dump these people, as they played important roles for me in other ways. But I needed to be more targeted in who I let influence my thinking."

Another overarching mistake we often see in executives' networks is an imbalance between connections that promote career advancement and those that promote engagement and satisfaction. Numerous studies have shown that happier executives are higher-performing ones.

Take Tim, the director of a large practice area at a leading professional services firm. On the surface he was doing well, but job stress had taken its toll. He was 40 pounds overweight, with alarmingly high cholesterol and blood sugar levels, and prone to extreme mood swings. When things went well at work, he was happy; when they didn't, he wasn't pleasant to be around. In fact, Tim's wife finally broke down and told him she thought he had become a career-obsessed jerk and needed to get other interests. With her encouragement, he joined Habitat for Humanity and started rowing with their daughter. As a result, his social network expanded to include people with different perspectives and values, who helped him focus on more healthful and fulfilling pursuits. "As I spent more time with different groups, what I cared about diversified," he says. "Physically, I'm in much better shape and probably staved off a heart attack. But I think I'm a better leader, too, in that I think about problems more broadly, and I'm more resilient. Our peer feedback systems are also clearly indicating that people are more committed to the new me."

Getting It Right

To understand more about what makes an effective network, let's look again at Deb. She has a small set of core contacts—14 people she really relies on. Effective core networks typically range in size from 12 to 18 people. But what really matters is structure: Core connections must bridge smaller, more-diverse kinds of groups and cross hierarchical, organizational, functional, and geographic lines. Core relationships should result in more learning, less bias in decision-making, and greater personal growth and balance. The people in your inner circle should also model positive behaviors, because if those around you are enthusiastic, authentic, and generous, you will be, too.

More specifically, our data show that high performers have strong ties to:

1. People who offer them new information or expertise, including internal or external clients, who increase their market awareness; peers in other functions, divisions, or geographies, who share best practices; and contacts in other industries, who inspire innovation;

2. Formally powerful people, who provide mentoring, sense-making, political support, and resources; and informally powerful people, who offer influence, help coordinating projects, and support among the rank and file; and

3. People who give them developmental feedback, challenge their decisions, and push them to be better. At an early career stage, an employee might get this from a boss or customers; later, it tends to come from coaches, trusted colleagues, or a spouse.

Four Steps to Building a Better Network

Analyze

Identify the people in your network and what you get out of interacting with them.

De-layer

Make some hard decisions to back away from redundant and energy-sapping relationships.

Diversify

Build your network out with the right kind of people: energizers who will help you achieve your goals.

Capitalize

Make sure you're using your contacts as effectively as you can.

Meanwhile, the most satisfied executives have ties to:

1. People who provide personal support, such as colleagues who help them get back on track when they're having a bad day or friends with whom they can just be themselves;

2. People who add a sense of purpose or worth, such as bosses and customers who validate their work, and family members and other stakeholders who show them work has a broader meaning; and

3. People who promote their work/life balance, holding them accountable for activities that improve their physical health (such as sports), mental engagement (such as

hobbies or educational classes), or spiritual well-being (music, religion, art, or volunteer work).

How does one create such a varied network? We recommend a four-point action plan: analyze, de-layer, diversify, and capitalize.

Analyze

Start by looking at the individuals in your network. Where are they located—are they within your team, your unit, or your company, or outside your organization? What benefits do your interactions with them provide? How energizing are those interactions?

The last question is an important one. Energizers bring out the best in everyone around them, and our data show that having them in your network is a strong predictor of success over time. These people aren't necessarily extroverted or charismatic. They're people who always see opportunities, even in challenging situations, and create room for others to meaningfully contribute. Good energizers are trustworthy and committed to principles larger than their self-interest, and they enjoy other people. "De-energizers," by contrast, are quick to point out obstacles, critique people rather than ideas, are inflexible in their thinking, fail to create opportunities, miss commitments, and don't show concern for others. Unfortunately, energy-sapping interactions have more impact than energizing ones—up to seven times as much, according to one study. And our own research suggests that roughly 90% of anxiety at work is created by 5% of one's network—the people who sap energy.

Next, classify your relationships by the benefits they provide. Generally, benefits fall into one of six basic categories: information, political support and influence, personal development, personal support and energy, a sense of purpose or worth, and work/life balance. It's important to have people who provide each kind of benefit in your network. Categorizing your relationships will give you a clearer idea of whether your network is extending your abilities or keeping you stuck. You'll see where you have holes and redundancies and which people you depend on too much—or not enough.

Let's use Joe, a rising star in an investment bank, as a case study. He had 24 close advisers—on the surface, a more than healthy number. But many of the people he relied on were from his own department and frequently relied on one another. If he eliminated those redundancies, his network shrank to five people. After giving it some thought and observing his peers' networks, he realized he was missing links with several important types of people: colleagues focused on financial offerings outside his own products, who could help him deliver broader financial solutions to customers; coworkers in different geographies—particularly London and Asia—who could enhance his ability to sell to global clients; and board-level relationships at key accounts, who could make client introductions and influence purchasing decisions. His insularity was limiting his options and hurting his chances of promotion to managing director. He realized he would need to focus on cultivating a network rather than allowing it to organically arise from the day-to-day demands of his work.

De-layer

Once you've analyzed your network, you need to make some hard decisions about which relationships to back away from. First, look at eliminating or minimizing contact with people who sap you of energy or promote unhealthful behaviors. You can do this by reshaping your role to avoid them, devoting less time to them, working to change their behavior, or reframing your reactions so that you don't dwell on the interactions.

John, an academic, realized that two university administrators in his network were causing him a great deal of anxiety. This had so soured his view of his school that he was considering leaving. He therefore decided to devote less time to projects and committees that would involve the negative contacts and to avoid dwelling on any sniping comments they subjected him to. Within a year he was much more productive and happy. "By shifting my role and how I reacted to the idiots, I turned a negative situation around," John says. "In hindsight it was an obvious move—rather than leave a place I loved—but emotions can spiral on you in ways you don't recognize."

The next step is to ask yourself which of the six categories have too many people in them. Early-stage leaders, for example, tend to focus too much on information and not enough on personal development and might want to shed some of the contacts who give them the former to make more time for those who give them the latter.

Beyond this, consider which individuals—and types of people as determined by function, hierarchy, or geography—have too much of you, and why. Is the cause structural, in that work procedures require you to be involved? Or is your own behavior causing the imbalance? What can you change to rectify the situation? Too often we see leaders fail because they accept or create too many collaborative demands.

Paul, the head of research in a consumer products company, had a network of almost 70 people just at work. But he got many complaints from people who said they needed greater access to him. His productivity, and his unit's, was suffering. When he analyzed his network, he realized that he was missing "people and initiatives one or two levels out." To address this, he decided to delegate—stepping away from interactions that didn't require his presence and cultivating "go to" stand-ins in certain areas of expertise. He also changed his leadership style from extraordinarily accessible to helpful but more removed, which encouraged subordinates to solve their own problems by connecting with people around him. "As a leader you can find yourself in this bubble of activity where you feel like a lot is happening moving from meeting to meeting," Paul says. "You can actually start to thrive on this in some ways. I had to move past this for us to be effective as a unit and so that I could be more forward-thinking."

Diversify

Now that you've created room in your network, you need to fill it with the right people. Simple tools like work sheets can help you get started. For example, you might make a list of the six categories of relationships and think about colleagues who could fill the holes you have in each. Remember to focus on positive, energetic, selfless people, and be sure to ask people inside and outside your network for recommendations.

You should also think about how you could connect your network to your professional and personal goals. Here's another simple exercise: Write down three specific business results you hope to achieve over the next year (such as doubling sales or winning an Asia-based client) and then list the people (by name or general role) who could help you with them, thanks to their expertise, control over resources, or ability to provide political support. Joe, the investment banker, identified counterparts in the Asian and European operations of his company who had relationships with the clients he was focused on and then scheduled regular calls with them to coordinate efforts. "In a couple of

Activate Your Network

by Deborah Grayson Riegel

Many folks think that networking is something you do only when you're looking for a job. But there are three important reasons you should always be working to keep your network active.

Use Your Network to Learn

We can all benefit from the wisdom, knowledge, and experience that our networks provide. While we're off living our lives, growing and learning, the people in our networks are doing the same. We're most likely to learn from our "dormant ties," or former colleagues and friends with whom we've lost touch. Reconnecting allows us to exchange information, share knowledge, and introduce one another to new skills.

- Build your network to supplement your knowledge of different industries and areas of expertise. Connect with people with diverse backgrounds and educations; people of genders, races, sexualities, and abilities different than your own; and people from different geographies, cultures, fields, and sectors.

- Offer your expertise to people who may want to learn from you in exchange for their advice and expertise, including areas beyond your professional realm. For instance, I'm not a travel agent, but my connections often tap me to help them plan trips since I'm well traveled. Similarly, I call one of my connections who's certified in mindfulness practices when I need a little emotional support.

- Reengage weak ties. Send an email to a former colleague, peer, professor, or friend with whom you've lost touch. It doesn't have to be complicated or apologetic. Say something like, "Hi there! I've been thinking about you and realized it's been a few years since we last connected. I would love to catch up at a time that works for you. Are you game?"

(continued)

Activate Your Network *(continued)*

Use Your Network to Help Others

So much of networking feels like asking for things, so offering your knowledge, skills, or expertise is a way to differentiate yourself and build deeper connections with people who may help grow your career later on. Helping others also triggers our reciprocity bias. When we help someone, they are more likely to help us in return.

- Consider how you might be helpful to your network beyond just making connections. Think about what you're good at, what you like to do, and what others often ask for your help with. This can range from listening empathetically to giving pep talks to helping someone celebrate a big win.

- Identify opportunities to help people in your network. Look for activities that, for you, are easy, rewarding, and satisfying, and don't require a lot of time. For example, if you're a great proofreader, and you can do it easily and quickly, offer to review the résumé and cover letter of a contact who's entering the job market.

- Play the long game. Think about your long-term career goals and identify people in your network who may be able to help you down the road. Now is the time to offer them help. For instance, perhaps you have a friend from college who is working in an industry you want to explore. Reach out to them to reconnect, check in, and ask what they might be looking for help with. Don't think of it as a quid pro quo. Consider it as an investment in your future relationship that may pay off.

Use Your Network to Sharpen Your Communication Skills

Networking allows us to strengthen skills that will help us in every other part of our careers by making us better problem-solvers, decision-makers, presenters, and communicators.

- Identify one or two communication skills you'd like to improve (such as listening without interrupting or describing what you do succinctly) and practice those skills during an upcoming networking conversation. Ask your connection for feedback.

- Have a conversation with someone in your network who holds different political, social, religious, or other viewpoints from your own. Practice having a respectful dialogue and exchange of ideas. Lead the conversation with curiosity.

- Practice your pitching skills by suggesting that your new connection meet with someone in your network. Tell a compelling story about how you met this other person, articulate why you think they'd be a good resource for your new connection, and ask if you can make an introduction. Then write a clear, concise, and compelling email introducing these two people.

Adapted from "Are You Taking Full Advantage of Your Network?" on hbr.org, November 28, 2022.

cases this helped me identify opportunities I could pitch proactively. In others it just helped us appear more coordinated when we were competing against other banks," he says. One of the big challenges for Paul, the consumer products executive, was managing a new facility and line of innovation in China. Because none of his trusted advisers had ever even been to that country, he reached out to the head of R&D at a major life-sciences organization that had undertaken a similar effort.

Capitalize

Last, make sure you're using your contacts as effectively as you can. Are there people you rely on in one sphere, such as political support, that you could also use to fill a need in another, such as personal development? Could you get more out of some relationships if you put more energy into them? Our research shows, for instance, that high performers at all levels tend to use their information contacts to gain other benefits, such as new ideas. Reciprocal relationships also tend to be more fruitful; the most successful leaders always look for ways to give more to their contacts.

Alan, a top executive at a global insurance company, realized that although he had a good network, he was still making decisions in relative isolation. He failed to elicit insights from others and, as a result, wasn't making enough progress toward his goals. So he started inviting his more-junior contacts, who were informal opinion leaders in his company, to lunch and asking them open-ended questions. These conversations led him to streamline decision-making and uncover innovation deep within the firm's hierarchy. "When I met with one lady, I was stunned at a great new product idea she had been pushing for months," Alan says. "But she hadn't been able to get the right people to listen. I was able to step in and help make things happen. To me the right way to be tapping into people is in this exploratory way— whether it is about strategic insights or just how they think I'm doing on some aspect of my job. That's how I get to new ways of thinking and doing things, and I know it makes me much more effective than people who are smarter than me."

A network constructed using this four-point model will build on itself over time. In due course, it will ensure that the best opportunities, ideas, and talent come your way.

Originally published in July–August 2011. Reprint R1107P

7

Beat Generosity Burnout

**by Adam Grant and
Reb Rebele**

When the leaders of the world dispense advice to the next generation, they tend to emphasize the same message: Help others. That was a key theme in almost two-thirds of graduation speeches at U.S. universities, according to one study.

Those who have "made it" promise graduates that being generous—readily sharing their time, energy, and expertise—will lead to a successful career and a meaningful, happy life. It can, but it doesn't always. The road to exhaustion is often paved with good intentions.

Four years ago one of us, Adam, published a book called *Give and Take*. It was about how generous "givers" succeed in ways that lift others up instead of cutting them down. It turned out that givers add more value to organizations than selfish "takers" or quid pro quo "matchers" do.

Givers do the lion's share of connecting, as in "Hey, Steve, you should meet my other friend Steve because you both love computers and playing pranks." (These two guys went on to found a company called Apple.) They stick their necks out to sponsor promising people and ideas: "I know this show is about nothing, and the characters aren't likable, but it made me laugh." (*Seinfeld* got another shot at NBC.) Givers share their knowledge freely: "You know your adhesive that won't stick? Why don't you use it to create a bookmark?" (Post-it notes were born.) And they volunteer to do the heavy lifting: "Sure, I'll take a crack at rewriting this script." (*Frozen* got the green light.)

Although givers are the most valuable people in organizations, they're also at the greatest risk for burnout. When they don't protect themselves, their investments in others can cause them to feel overloaded and fatigued, fall behind on their work goals, and face more stress and conflict at home.[1]

Adam's book made the case that givers can rise to the top, but it scratched only the surface on the question of how. We've spent the past four years studying what givers can do to sustain their energy—and their effectiveness. That's what we'll discuss here, after we look at how well-meaning but overly altruistic people get in their own way.

When Good Intentions Go Wrong

Givers at the top are often called servant leaders. They selflessly put the needs of others first, and that helps drive their firms' success: A study of technology companies revealed that when CFOs agreed with statements like "The CEO seems to care more about the organization's success than their own," their firms had significantly higher returns on assets in the follow-

Idea in Brief

The Problem

Selflessness at work leads to exhaustion—and often hurts the very people you want to help. As a high performer your name is at the top of everyone's list when they consider who can help them with a project or an issue. When you're generous with your time and talents, you can face significant stress and burnout as you both offer support to others and work on your own goals.

The Solution

To combat generosity burnout, you need to set boundaries. When you manage your time and energy more effectively, you can sustain your ability to help others without depleting yourself. Be strategic about when and how to help others, prioritize tasks, and learn to say no when necessary.

The Benefits

By taking these steps to protect yourself, you can share your time and expertise more effectively. You can be generous while maintaining your own well-being and productivity without feeling overloaded and fatigued.

ing quarter—relative both to other firms and to their own past performance.[2]

You want the top boss to put the organization first. But do you also want everyone else to be selfless?

To find out, we've been studying people in a wide range of jobs. Some of our favorite recent data points come from more than 400 second-year teachers (from pre-K through high school) throughout the United States. At the start of the year we asked them a series of questions about their approach to helping. Their answers allowed us to predict how well their students would do on end-of-year academic achievement tests.

Here's a sample question:

Imagine that you're teaching a geometry class, and you've volunteered to stay after school one day a week to help one of your students, Alex, improve his understanding of geometry. He asks if you'll also help his friend Juan, who isn't in your class. What would you do?

   a. Schedule a separate after-school session to help Juan so that you can better understand his individual needs.

   b. Invite Juan to sit in on your geometry sessions with Alex.

   c. Tell Alex that it's nice that he wants to help Juan, but he really needs to focus on his own work in order to catch up.

   d. Tell Alex that Juan should ask his own teacher for help.

Teaching is a helping profession, so we knew we'd find plenty of highly motivated givers. We wanted to see how much they would sacrifice themselves. We gave them 11 scenarios—some with requests from students; others with requests from fellow teachers or administrators. The more times teachers chose option (a), the worse their students performed.

Option (a) is what we call a selfless response—helping without boundaries. Compared with their self-protective peers, selfless teachers saw significantly lower student achievement scores on standardized assessments at the end of the year. This effect was especially pronounced for teachers whose students had performed poorly the previous year. Selfless educators exhausted themselves trying to help everyone with every request. They were willing to work nights and weekends to assist students with problems, colleagues with lesson plans, and principals with administrative duties. Despite their best intentions, these teachers were inadvertently hurting the very students they wanted to help.

This kind of dilemma isn't unique to teaching. As we wrote in an HBR article with Rob Cross last year, collaborative overload is pervasive in workplaces around the world, and selfless givers are its biggest victims. Employees who consistently demonstrate the motivation and ability to lend a hand get "rewarded" with the bulk of requests and often find themselves drowning in meetings and emails. The result is that they are at risk of burnout or attrition, their colleagues are frustrated by a lack of access to the help they need, and other employees who could be pitching in are instead sitting idle and disengaged.

Meanwhile, our research shows that across industries the people who make the most sustainable contributions to organizations—those who offer the most direct support, take the most initiative, and make the best suggestions—protect their time so that they can work on their own goals, too.[3]

People often make the mistake of confusing generosity with selflessness. As the writer Caroline McGraw observes, "We've been conditioned to believe that being kind means being available 24/7."[4] Being an effective giver isn't about dropping everything every time for every person. It's about making sure that the benefits of helping others outweigh the costs to you. Finding ways to give without depleting your time and energy—as in option (b) in the sample question—is generous but not selfless. The teachers who took that approach didn't see their performance suffer the way their peers who consistently went way above and beyond did.

Effective givers recognize that every *no* frees you up to say yes when it matters most. After all, it's hard to support others when you're so overloaded that you've hit a wall. As comedian George Carlin put it, "They tell you to adjust *your* oxygen mask before

Where Are You on the Generosity Spectrum?

And where are your colleagues?

Takers see every interaction as an opportunity to advance their own interests. They will run you ragged if you don't protect yourself. But you can get better at spotting takers if you know what clues to look for: They act as if they deserve your help, and they don't hesitate to impose on your time.

Matchers trade favors evenly. They can give as good as they get, but they expect reciprocity. Matching is a transactional, defensive stance—it adds less value for both you and others, but it can be helpful when you're dealing with a taker.

Self-protective givers are generous, but they know their limits. Instead of saying yes to every help request, they look for high-impact, low-cost ways of giving so that they can sustain their generosity—and enjoy it along the way.

Selfless givers have high concern for others but low concern for themselves. They set few or no boundaries, which makes them especially vulnerable to takers. By ignoring their own needs, they exhaust themselves and, paradoxically, end up helping others less.

helping your child with his. *I* did not need to be told that! . . . This will be a good time for him to learn self-reliance."

We've discovered that productive giving comes in three flavors: being thoughtful about *how* you help, *when* you help, and *whom* you help.

How to Help: Jack-of-All-Trades, Stuck with a Ton

Ad hoc requests for help are among the biggest drains on people's energy and time. When we studied managers, engineers, and salespeople at a *Fortune* 500 technology company, more than

60% said they would like to spend significantly less time in "responding" mode. And other research suggests that 75% to 90% of all the helping in organizations is reactive: Someone makes a request, and we respond.[5] Great to meet you, burnout.

In a new study, researchers surveyed managerial and professional employees every day for three workweeks.[6] The more times people responded to help requests from coworkers on a particular day, the more their energy was depleted—and the more trouble they had focusing their attention and persisting with difficult tasks. This effect lasted until the next morning, and it was especially strong for givers who'd made sacrifices to go the extra mile for their colleagues.

Reactive helping is exhausting, but proactive giving can be energizing. We've seen this with Adam Rifkin, who has been recognized as *Fortune*'s best networker for having an unusually high number of ties to powerful people. Rifkin is a computer programmer who founded a series of technology startups and did well enough to retire in his thirties. As word spread of his generosity and success as an entrepreneur, he was bombarded with requests for business plan advice. ("Dear Mr. Rifkin: I know we've never met, but I was wondering if you would read my 274-page business plan and then meet with me for coffee to discuss . . .")

Rifkin didn't have time to meet with everyone who asked, and he didn't particularly enjoy dispensing business plan advice. So he decided to start giving on his own terms. He had a knack for matchmaking—connecting strangers was his favorite way to help others. One morning he set a goal: Every day he would make three introductions between people who could benefit from knowing each other. He did that for the next decade, making more than 10,000 introductions and opening doors that allowed hundreds of people to find jobs and dozens to launch companies. He also accidentally arranged a couple of marriages: He told people, "Hey, I think you two would hit it off professionally," and then—whoops—they fell in love.

As Rifkin started making introductions, he noticed that the business plan requests dropped off. Before, he'd had a reputation as a nice guy, someone who would help anyone with anything. He was stuck responding to the full suite of requests that flooded his inbox. Now he was known as a great connector. People started taking their miscellaneous requests elsewhere, because why would you go to *Fortune*'s top networker for business plan advice when the best resource he can offer you is an introduction?

We all can be more thoughtful about how we help. Building on a nationally representative poll of Americans, we've found six profiles of giving:[7]

- *Experts* share knowledge.

- *Coaches* teach skills.

- *Mentors* give advice and guidance.

- *Connectors* make introductions.

- *Extra-milers* show up early, stay late, and volunteer for extra work.

- *Helpers* provide hands-on task support and emotional support.

Don't try to be everything to everyone. Cast your eyes over this list and think about what makes sense for you. Identify two or three ways of offering unique value to others—things you do well and enjoy.

As giving aligns with your interests and skills, it becomes less stressful for you and more valuable to others. Rather than feeling pressured to help, you're choosing to help, which is good for your motivation, creativity, and well-being.[8] Instead of being known as a jack-of-all-trades, you're seen as a master of a few. That frees you up to focus on helping where you have the most impact—which replenishes your energy by reminding you how much your contributions matter. It gives you license to turn down requests that aren't in your wheelhouse, because you have a track record of helping. And it allows you to make choices about when to step up.

When to Help: It's About Time

Ryan Daly served as an army lieutenant in Iraq, surviving an ambush and losing four men in 15 months. Upon leaving the military, he went to business school and made a personal commitment to help others with their career transitions. Soon he was fielding 40 calls a month from veterans. As word spread of his generosity, the requests for advice ballooned. By the time Daly started his full-time job in advertising at Google, he was averaging nearly a hundred of those conversations a month.

He thought about sending out an FAQ document but decided that wouldn't work. "It's very important that I get back to everyone in a timely manner," Daly told us. "But I want to give people something tailored to them." He didn't know how he could do both.

We suggested that Daly set up a weekly Google hangout. When people reached out, he would send them a link to sign up for it. That way, he could still interact with them directly, but he could also answer common questions in fewer conversations. He was able to help more people and feel less depleted.

As Daly had discovered, giving becomes a grind when it takes over your time. For some people—like those at the technology company we studied—a high volume of low-value requests eats into time that could be used for greater productivity or impact. For others—like the teachers mentioned earlier—going all-in on many individual help requests leads to working long nights and weekends instead of resting or pursuing personal enrichment or development. Either way, protecting your calendar is essential to sustaining generosity.

That doesn't necessarily mean spending less time helping; it can be more about pacing yourself and allocating your time wisely. In one of our favorite experiments, psychologists asked people to perform five random acts of kindness every week for six weeks.[9] Participants were randomly assigned to either "sprinkling" or "chunking" their acts of kindness. Sprinkling meant spreading them out by doing one a day. Chunking meant picking one day—let's say Thursday—for all five helpful acts.

Half the participants experienced a boost in happiness and energy that lasted for the entire study. For the other half, the giving did nothing whatsoever to improve their moods. When we asked executives to guess which group got the energy spike, more than 80% voted for sprinkling. They assumed that a little giving every day is a reliable way to lift your spirits. But they're wrong. Only the chunking group got happier.

One act of helping a day does nothing for your mood because it's a drop in the bucket. A distracting blip. But if you help five people every Thursday, you feel you've made a difference each week. And you have more flexibility to make progress in your own work the rest of the time.

Of course, it isn't practical to organize every week or every act of generosity like this. But we can all do better at timing our giving to manage our energy. In one study of salespeople, helping others meant lower performance for people with poor time

Seven Habits of Highly Productive Giving

1. Prioritize the help requests that come your way—say yes when it matters most and no when you need to.

2. Give in ways that play to your interests and strengths to preserve your energy and provide greater value.

3. Distribute the giving load more evenly—refer requests to others when you don't have the time or skills, and be careful to not reinforce gender biases about who helps and how.

4. Secure your oxygen mask first—you'll help others more effectively if you don't neglect your own needs.

5. Amplify your impact by looking for ways to help multiple people with a single act of generosity.

6. Chunk your giving into dedicated days or blocks of time rather than sprinkling it throughout the week. You'll be more effective—and more focused.

7. Learn to spot takers, and steer clear of them. They're a drain on your energy, not to mention a performance hazard.

management skills but higher performance for those with excellent time management skills.[10]

One effective tactic is batching common requests, as Daly did with his Google hangouts. Along with being more efficient for him, this approach was more beneficial for the veterans: Many of them felt alone in their transition to civilian work, and the hangouts made them part of a community.

Another strategy is to create a personal library of useful responses and resources. How many times have you written different versions of the same email from scratch? Certain types of questions are bound to come up more often than others. Sending someone an FAQ may feel too impersonal, but that doesn't mean you need to completely personalize every response. When you take the time to explain something clearly or to put together a list of useful resources on a certain topic, why should only one person benefit? Copying the most relevant sections to a document saves time and expands the return on your initial investment.

There are other ways to streamline the giving process. Professors schedule office hours to make themselves available to students and set aside separate windows for work on their own research. This may not be a great idea with your boss or your direct reports, but you can use office hours to keep your work time from being overrun by random meetings. We both use online scheduling tools to manage requests for meetings and calls outside our core responsibilities. This allows us to draw boundaries around our availability instead of declaring open season on our calendars. And it saves back-and-forth emailing to find a time that works—something people reaching out usually appreciate just as much as we do.

Of course, no matter how efficiently you manage the giving pipeline, you may still get more demands than you can meet. How can you decide who really needs and deserves your time?

Whom to Help: Hint—Not Everyone

Callie Schweitzer rose rapidly through the ranks of digital media. Just a few years out of college she began running marketing and communications at Vox Media and soon was leading audience strategy across Time Inc. She quickly faced a barrage of requests, from students seeking career advice or wanting to profile her for class papers to journalists looking for insights about communications. The week she was transitioning to a new job, a student on a class deadline got in touch with her, wanting to talk right away. Schweitzer explained that she was too swamped for a call on short notice but would be happy to answer a specific question by email. The student followed up with six in-depth questions, asking for extensive explanations. Essentially, he was requesting that Schweitzer write the paper—on the future of journalism, no less—for him.

The bad news is that givers are vulnerable to takers. They tend to trust too readily and see the best in everyone. But that can actually make them better lie detectors, research shows. Because they trust others, they are lied to more often. Givers get to see the full spectrum of human behavior. If they pay close attention, they can learn to recognize the clues that reveal selfishness: Acting entitled to people's help. Claiming credit for success while blaming others for failure. Kissing up and kicking down. Being nice to your face and then stabbing you in the back—or being nice only when seeking a favor. Overpromising and underdelivering. As David Aikman at the World Economic Forum puts it, "There are talker-takers and giver-doers."

Spend enough time with someone, and these patterns tend to reveal themselves. But as we've already seen, time is not something givers can spare. If it takes weeks or months to realize someone is taking advantage of your generosity, you've already paid the price—and so have all the other people who really needed your help.

To prevent generosity burnout, you have to hone your skill at prioritizing requests and screening for sincerity. The most successful givers act like triage nurses in an emergency room: When someone comes along asking for help, they don't jump straight into a treatment plan. Instead they gather information to determine how serious and urgent the need is, figure out who the best person to help might be, and assess whether any small remedies would be useful in the meantime. Only then do they decide how—or even whether—to help. As Caroline McGraw reminds us, "You don't owe anyone an interaction."

What are some other early clues that you might be dealing with a taker? Consider how the request for help is made. Givers recognize that asking for help is an imposition on your time, and they go out of their way to make it as easy as possible for you to respond. They ask for five-minute favors and offer to work around your schedule. Takers, on the other hand, contact you out of the blue and ask if you can "jump on a call today," follow up multiple times if you don't respond right away, and insist on meeting on their terms even though they're the ones imposing on you.

Another sign is that when you give an inch, they try to take a mile. Givers respond to help with gratitude and a willingness to pay it forward. If they follow up, they do so cautiously and without expectations. Takers treat help as an open invitation to get more of the same. That's how collaborative overload creeps in: What you thought was a one-off request to share some information slowly turns into an ongoing commitment to someone else's project.

When you're dealing with people who have a history of selfishness, don't reinforce their behavior by being too generous. Approach them the way "matchers" would: Ask them to reciprocate or help others. And if you have a real relationship with the other party, it may be time for a difficult conversation.

Early in her career, Schweitzer felt compelled to say yes to every request. By the time the student sent his six questions, she had learned to set limits. She answered one of the questions. He never responded.

Mind the Gender Gap

People often ask us if generosity burnout differs based on gender. When we analyzed the data, we were saddened to learn that, as you might assume, men are more likely to be takers and women are more likely to be selfless givers. It happens in workplaces around the world: Women are expected to do more of the helping, but they get less of the credit for it.

In her studies of gender differences in the workplace, Simmons researcher Joyce Fletcher observed that dynamic in action. At one technology company, a major product launch was on the verge of falling apart until a group of female design engineers saved it. They took the initiative to fix shoddy products before they were shipped. They translated technical jargon so that coworkers could understand it, taught less experienced colleagues how to address computer problems, and jumped in when their peers refused to help. They resolved conflicts between teammates, listened to frustrations, and offered advice and encouragement.

When these women swooped in to help their team, they should have been rewarded. But they weren't. No one really noticed. When a female engineer showed a faulty product to the male quality control manager, he shrugged, so she took it upon herself to come in on a Saturday to fix it. "The manager did not thank her," Fletcher writes, "or give any verbal or nonverbal affirmation."[11] When the men did acknowledge the women's help, they often dismissed it because it appeared to threaten their own feelings of competence. In four years of shadowing and interviewing the team, Fletcher saw this happen over and over. For the female engineers, helping was a disappearing act.

Women shoulder responsibility for the giving acts that are most valuable but least visible, like mentoring behind the scenes.[12] They get stuck with the office housework—planning meetings, taking notes. And they don't get that time back to use for their own work, professional development, or opportunities to volunteer for higher-visibility initiatives.

If we want to stop generosity burnout, we need to shift the balance. For women, that means setting boundaries instead of being selfless. For the men who work with them, it means stepping up to do more of the helping and mentoring. For organizations, it means assigning and evaluating work on the basis of people's contributions, not their gender. And for all of us, it means that it's high time to stop reserving the generosity glory for men and dumping the grunt work of giving on women.

. . .

Although giving makes our jobs and our lives more meaningful, it doesn't always make us more energized. On average, helping others makes people only modestly happier—and in some studies, takers actually report more pleasure in life than givers.[13] It's not hard to figure out why. When people are selfless to the point of burnout, they undermine their own ability to give and the satisfaction that comes from it.

Generosity means caring about others, but not at the expense of caring for yourself. By protecting yourself from exhaustion, you may feel less altruistic. Yet, you will actually end up giving more.

Adapted from hbr.org, January 23, 2017. Reprint H03EZX

The Talent Curse

**by Jennifer Petriglieri and
Gianpiero Petriglieri**

T
here were many late nights during Thomas's time at a private equity firm, but two of them really stand out. On the first, he was at a bar. Earlier in the day, his boss had let him know that he was the top performer in his cohort. Over drinks that evening, he struck up a conversation with a partner at a rival firm. "You're the guy who closed two deals in six months, aren't you?" the man asked. It was a moment Thomas had dreamed of and worked for since leaving his small town for college, the first in his family, years before.

On the second, he was at his desk, working on a high-profile IPO. He was the only associate on the deal—the kind of assignment reserved for top talent on the firm's fast track to partnership. Dawn was breaking, and he had no memory of the past six hours, even though his email and phone logs chronicled a busy all-nighter. A neurologist later ran some tests and warned him of the dangers of sleep deprivation. "I would go to bed at five, wake up at seven with palpitations, and go to work,"

Thomas recalled. "I never stopped to think that it was wrong. It's how it works, I told myself. Everyone does it."

Thomas slowed down briefly after the doctor's warning but soon came back full throttle. His talent and drive were intact, though somehow he'd lost his sense of purpose. He created an opportunity for the firm to do a $1.3 billion deal, and then surprised his bosses by suddenly quitting. His performance was strong and his prospects bright as ever, but as he put it when we spoke, he had fallen victim to a vicious cycle: "I did not want to step off the fast track, so I could not slow down." Thomas felt trapped by his firm's expectations, but his desire to prove deserving of his bosses' endorsement kept him from challenging the culture or asking for support. He felt both overwhelmed and underutilized, and concluded that this firm was not the right place to realize his leadership ambitions.

In our two decades of studying and working with "future leaders" like Thomas, we've met many people who struggle with what appears to be their good fortune. In most cases, these managers and professionals have been accurately identified as star performers and fast learners. But often, placement on a fast track doesn't speed up their growth as leaders in the organization, as it's meant to do. Instead, it either pushes them out the door or slows them down—thwarting their development, decreasing their engagement, and hurting their performance.

In an age when companies wage wars for talent, it is hard to acknowledge that for some people, being recognized as talented turns out to be a curse. But it does. Aspiring leaders work hard to live up to others' expectations, and so the qualities that made them special to begin with—those that helped them excel and feel engaged—tend to get buried. They behave more

Idea in Brief

The Problem

When people are groomed as future leaders, they often feel trapped by others' expectations and fixate on proving themselves worthy. Sometimes they end up blandly conforming to their organization's established leadership ideal and losing their edge. Sometimes they leave altogether, depriving themselves of an opportunity and the organization of their talent.

The Remedy

High potentials struggle with this "talent curse" again and again as they take on new roles and challenges. But they can grow from the experience by accepting the help they need to thrive, bringing all facets of themselves to the job (not just those that say "leadership material"), and treating the present like a final destination.

like everyone else, which saps their energy and ambition. They may start simply going through the motions at work—or, like Thomas, look for an escape hatch.

This curse strikes the talented even in companies that invest heavily in their development—places where executives are sincerely dedicated to helping people thrive. We began to notice it long ago, when one of us (Jennifer) worked in various multinationals and the other (Gianpiero) practiced as a psychotherapist in a global MBA program. Since then, we've studied hundreds of managers and professionals from various sectors and parts of the world—many of whom we have followed over time—and met thousands more in our teaching, consulting, and coaching engagements. Through that work with high potentials, we've examined talent development from their perspective and identified common psychological dynamics, signs of trouble, and ways of breaking the curse.

The Psychology Behind the Curse

Often, the curse begins when an organization gives an employee a platform to hone his or her skills in hopes of earning some reward, such as partnership, a senior leadership position, or just a broader range of career options. Although that person is flattered and grateful at first, a resentful angst eventually sets in—a feeling that's difficult to explain or justify. It's not garden-variety uncertainty, which you'd expect of anyone facing new challenges; the roots reach much deeper, into the self.

Two psychological mechanisms, idealization and identification, turn out to be a destructive combination for high potentials: Others idealize their talent as a defense against the company's uncertain future, and then the high potentials identify with that image, shouldering the uncertainty themselves.[1] That's what happened to Thomas. After his early successes brokering deals, his bosses and colleagues began to see him as a rainmaker the firm could rely on in the volatile PE world. The combination of idealization and identification is evident in many workplaces where people praise the promise of the talented, and the talented feel the burden of their promise. If the future isn't as bright as everyone hoped, it will be they who have failed.

As their talent increasingly defines them, high potentials sense that their own future is at stake too. They fixate on what they should do to ensure their place in the organization. Though these expectations might be amplified in their minds, they aren't simply self-imposed. They're spelled out in lists of company values and competencies, which up-and-coming leaders are meant to model, and reinforced through performance feedback and informal interactions.

Lars, a rising star at a manufacturing company, explained it like this at a leadership workshop: "One day I'm told that those like me must transform the way we do business; the next day, that I must make sure that the executives whose business I must transform appreciate me."

We often hear this sort of thing. In companies whose executives want strong cultures and rapid change, talented managers feel pressured both to be revolutionaries and to win the establishment's approval. The inherent tension between those pursuits wears people down. Their sensitivity to cultural and political cues—part of the reason they've been flagged as future leaders—makes them especially vulnerable once they're on that track.

Every opportunity becomes an obligation; every challenge, a test. The high potential strives to be a perfect manager, now suppressing the very talents—the passions and idiosyncrasies—that made her stand out in the first place. And so the curse twists talent management against its intent. Rather than empowering those who deserve to lead, it increases their insecurity and pushes them to conform, like a protection racket of sorts—a company's costly demands in exchange for safety from the threats that working there presents. "Future leader" becomes a synonym for "exceptional follower."

Three Signs of Trouble

You must have high standards for yourself and be ready for extra scrutiny—no aspiring leader can ignore others' expectations. But you can shine only so long under the spotlight of opportunity and the magnifying glass of expectations before burning out—unless you put some protections in place. That requires learning to spot and deal with three signs of trouble.

1. A shift from simply using your talent to proving it

After being placed in a high-potential pool, you may find that your excitement about the recognition soon fades, whereas the new expectations create ongoing pressure. That's what typically happens. Caught between the acknowledgment of their past achievements and the possibility of future opportunities, aspiring leaders often view the present as a time to prove that they deserve both. In an effort to ensure that they fulfill their promise, they become more calculating about where and how they apply themselves.

Companies with a formal high-potential track aren't the only places where this happens. In some organizations, senior executives just take an interest in certain employees, and things snowball from there. Take Laura, who left halfway through a PhD program in artificial intelligence to try her hand in the business world. Laura joined a consultancy and then moved on to a role in the strategy function of a consumer goods company. About a year into that new job, her boss's boss recognized her skills in data analytics. So he brokered an introduction that led Laura into a role managing digital marketing for one of the company's floundering products.

"It was as if everything came together in that moment," Laura told us. Her understanding of data analytics and her experience in business strategy made her a great fit for the job. All she had to do now was deliver. Succeeding in her new role, the hiring executive assured her, would "open every door in this industry." The pressure was on.

Laura then fell into a spiral of overwork, anxious to show others—and herself—that she could handle the challenge. Although sales grew, she felt that no one noticed her dedication and results. Perhaps, she thought, her work wasn't impressive enough. "I feared that people were nice to me," she said, "but didn't have the guts to tell me that maybe I had plateaued, that my time was up." This was hardly what others thought. Accustomed to her competent and composed demeanor, her bosses and colleagues assumed that she needed little help. And they were more than happy to let her carry on, praising her independence and initiative without realizing the struggle beneath both.

In her seminal research, Stanford psychologist Carol Dweck has drawn a distinction between a performance orientation and a learning orientation.[2] When children believe that their intelligence is a fixed quantity, she found, they tend to become easily discouraged by tough school assignments and give up quickly on the problems they cannot easily solve. Children who sense that their intelligence is malleable, conversely, stay on those problems longer, seeing them as a way to keep improving. Those with a performance orientation are embarrassed by failure, whereas those with a learning orientation are spurred on by it—they work harder. The same is true for adults at work, Dweck found.

The amplified expectations that high potentials internalize are a classic circumstance that, Dweck's research predicts, will elicit a performance orientation. Though Laura and many others we have studied didn't give up on hard challenges or stop striving to develop their skills, their learning itself became a performance of sorts—a way of affirming their talent. As a result, extra experiments and side projects—which could further expand their skills but also reveal their flaws—began to feel like risks they could not afford.

This is how special people become ordinary. After being placed on the partnership track at a global firm, one consultant recalled, "I knew I could succeed, so I focused on where I knew my talents shone. It was great in the short term, but over time I began to lose my edge."

The pressure is even stronger for minorities, who may also feel obligated to serve as role models and advocates for those whose talent often goes unseen. Consider how a female junior partner in a male-dominated elite law firm changed her mindset after finding out she was in the running to become an equity partner. "I have no doubt that I deserve a place at the table," she told us, "but I feel totally paralyzed. I am being very conservative because I feel that if I fail at anything, I will let everyone down." She knew she was a role model for other women, which raised the stakes even more. Rather than expand her expertise, she stuck to areas where she knew she would perform well and to clients with whom she had established relationships. When she was not able to bring in the number of new clients expected from an equity partner, her career progress slowed.

2. A preoccupation with image despite a yearning for authenticity

An investment banker who ended up leaving his firm told us, "I was always in the spotlight, always performing, always trying to be the leader they expected me to be." Though he had worked very hard to get to that visible position, once on the fast track, he felt strangely invisible. It was as if the firm had hijacked his identity along with his ambition. As he put it, "No one saw the real me."

The preoccupation with image is a natural consequence of the pressure to prove one's talent—and it's a common problem, our INSEAD colleague Herminia Ibarra has found in her research on leadership transitions.[3] At most firms, the promise of future leadership is bestowed on those who conform to the desired organizational culture—the values and vision established by those at the top. So while many companies invite employees to "bring themselves" to work, people on a high-potential track often bring only those aspects that say "leadership material"—and this makes them feel inauthentic.

This isn't a problem just for those uncomfortable with "faking it" until they acquire new leadership skills—which, as Ibarra argues, can actually help people discover new facets of themselves. It can also happen to people who take on roles that seem like a natural fit. Laura, the data scientist, could easily put forward the problem-solving, data-driven self that her company valued. But there was more to her than that. No matter how fitting the role, when people continually display just one aspect of themselves, it flattens and limits them. That happened to Laura. By being true to just part of her identity—on demand—she lost her sense of ownership and spontaneity.

Like many others caught in this position, Laura considered leaving and fantasized about getting a job where she would be "free to be myself." In one study we conducted with CEIBS professor Jack Wood, in which we followed a cohort of MBAs for a year, nearly half the participants said that they sought a similar escape. They hoped business school would provide a retreat—a space where they could discover and recover who they really were.

In her classic research, psychologist Alice Miller examined what she provocatively labeled "the drama of the gifted child."[4] She described how inquisitive and intelligent children often learn to hide their feelings and needs to meet their doting parents' expectations. They do this so well that over time they no longer know what they feel and need. The sense of emptiness and alienation that Miller chronicled resembles what we have encountered among high-potential managers: Paradoxically, being recognized as talented robs them of their talents. Their talents still exist but are no longer their own; they belong to a distant and demanding organizational "parent."

3. Postponement of meaningful work

When people feel trapped by their organization's expectations and anticipate great rewards for enduring that captivity with dignity, the present loses meaning for them. They begin to locate their dreams for recovering and expressing themselves in the future—when they will finally, they hope, be free to say what they mean, relate to others openly, fulfill their true calling, and lead as they have wanted to all along.

Some just wait for the numbness to dissipate. Others harbor flourishing images of what they will do once they've quit the rat race—goals they share with only a few trusted friends for fear that those dreams, too, might be hijacked. This amounts to what Jungian analyst H.G. Baynes labeled, long ago, the "neurosis of the provisional life": While developing leaders view their current work as instrumental to future opportunities, they imagine that their future work will be much more meaningful. Who they will be becomes more important than who they are. The present loses value, so they stop giving their best.

By the time the engaged self escapes to the future, the talent curse has taken hold. While the high potential might appear immersed in her work, she is sealed off from it. And if she continues to view her present work as empty, not even leaving the organization will help. In the study we mentioned earlier, people who had begun an MBA program in search of a retreat found themselves caught in the same spiral of striving to meet expectations that they resented, and dreaming of other escapes. "Every day I woke up and wanted to leave," one participant recalled. "I wanted to go and tell no one."

Another explained how he began to second-guess his past choices. "When I finished my undergraduate degree," he recalled, "I got arguably the most enviable job in my class, and of course I took it. It was the prestigious thing to do. I never really sat back and thought, Do I really want to do this?" He was hoping to transition out—somehow. He didn't know where he'd go, but he imagined that almost any option must be better than where he was.

When Laura told us her story, she talked about maybe returning to finish her PhD—immediately after wondering if she could be a COO one day. It was as if the thought of another step in her career progression demanded a counterthought of escape, a way out for the self from a job she excelled at and an organization that valued her work.

Breaking the Talent Curse

Though the curse can hamper the personal growth, engagement, and career progress of the most gifted high potentials, it can be broken. We recommend three steps:

1. Own your talent—don't be possessed by it

Once your talent becomes your identity, every challenge to it (there will be plenty if you are stretching to learn) feels like a challenge to the self. As Laura put it when one peer questioned her ability, "It struck me to my core." Slavishly bowing to everyone's expectations, including your own, is no solution; you'll just become a follower of what you believe others want. Nor is ignoring those expectations; at best, you will be seen as a rebel.

Instead, remain mindful of what you need and what others want—without allowing either to consume you.

Striking that balance often involves learning how to accept help, even when you don't think you need it, rather than going it alone. This is something that Michael Sanson, an executive coach at INSEAD, emphasizes with his clients. "A key shift occurs," he says, "when a high potential realizes that his or her role is not to deliver more than others, but to deliver more *with* others." People sometimes resist feedback and coaching, he explains, because they view both as vehicles for more expectations. When they begin to see the input not as judgment but as a source of support, they become great listeners and fast learners—which helps them perform better and grow as leaders.

2. Bring your whole self, not just your best self, to work

It's tempting to show only the shiny, polished facets of ourselves—especially when we value them and others appreciate them. But our greatest talents often spring from wounds and quirks, from the rougher, less conformist sides of ourselves. Much resolve flows from restlessness, creativity from angst, and resilience from having faced challenges we'd rather not share. Managers who are empathetic (and thus great with people) sometimes get overwhelmed by emotions. Don't fight these darker sources of your talent. Learn to channel them.

The last time we spoke to Thomas, the former private equity associate, he was transitioning into the field of talent management. He brought his business acumen to it, but also a deep personal understanding of how organizations can boost or hinder employees' growth, and vice versa. His firsthand struggle to develop and thrive at his old firm gave him insight that allowed him to help others develop and thrive. He was no longer just gifted. He was purposeful and revitalized.

3. Value the present

This is the most important step in breaking the curse. Ask yourself: What if this is it? What if my current work is not a stepping-stone, but a destination? You must invest in the work you're doing now—make it matter—in order to grow from the experience.

Look at the expectations, the pressures, and the doubts you face as challenges that all leaders face. They aren't tests for leadership; they are features of leading. They won't go away once you prove yourself worthy—they'll only intensify. So now is the time to muster the resources you'll need to manage them over the long run. And accept that even with plenty of resources, leading will always require courage. As Mette Stuhr, a former head of talent management at a multinational corporation who has taught and coached scores of high potentials all over the world, puts it: "If you wait for it to be safe to speak up, you never will."

A Rite of Passage

For all the pain it causes and the risks it entails, the talent curse is a rite of passage. Breaking the curse is an important part of learning how to lead. And it's an ongoing process—high potentials must do this again and again as they grow into new roles.

Let's return to Laura's example: During a team retreat, she finally took the plunge and confessed that she was thinking about leaving. In a well-rehearsed argument, she explained how the structure of her department was creating friction between her and two peers. Much to her surprise, what she thought might become a farewell speech was very well received. Voicing her concerns paid off. The structure changed. She stayed.

Soon after that, Laura was offered a bigger role leading a team of five managers, with 52 people below them. She felt energized at first, because she could have an impact on the whole company. But then new doubts started gnawing at her—and again, she asked for no support. Six months into the new role, she had not yet negotiated her package. "I got a great job," she said. "What would they think if I worried about the contract, the salary, and things like that?" Upholding her image as a passionate go-getter prevented her from making arrangements to succeed. "I have not yet proved myself," she said. "How can I ask for more? I should be grateful."

Once more, an opportunity turned into a burden, and Laura became sad and frustrated. Neither her boss nor her organization had intended any of this. They had been happy to give a stretch assignment to an ambitious and responsible young manager. They did not maliciously withdraw support, but they didn't encourage her to seek it, either. They never invited her to take it a little easier or told her that she shouldn't expect to get everything right. And so they reinforced her modus operandi.

That brings us to our final point: Organizations should do their part to break the curse too. They should stop referring to talented young managers as "future leaders," since it encourages bland conformity, risk-averse thinking, and stilted behavior. They should stop offering responsibility in the present with the promise of authority later on. And they should allow people room to deviate from the image of leadership that others have drawn. That will ease the pressure for managers to prove their talent, freeing them to simply use it—to engage with their work and grow into better leaders.

The best way to develop leaders, in the end, is to help them lead. The best way to learn to lead is to accept that help in the here and now.

Originally published in May–June 2017. Reprint R1703E

Sleep Well, Lead Better

by Christopher M. Barnes

How much sleep do you get each night? Most of us know that eight hours is the recommended amount, but with work, family, and social commitments often consuming more than 16 hours of the day, it can seem impossible to make the math work. Perhaps you feel that you operate just fine on four or five hours a night. Maybe you've grown accustomed to red-eye flights, time zone changes, and the occasional all-nighter. You might even wear your sleep deprivation like a badge of honor.

If this sounds familiar, you're not alone. Although the ranks of sleep advocates are no doubt growing—led by the likes of Arianna Huffington and Jeff Bezos—a significant percentage of people, and U.S. executives in particular, don't seem to be getting the sleep they need. According to the most recent data from the National Health Interview Survey, the proportion of Americans getting no more than six hours a night (the minimum for a good night's rest for most people) rose from 22% in 1985 to 29% in 2012. An international study conducted in 2017 by the Center for Creative Leadership found that among leaders, the problem is even worse: 42% get six or fewer hours of shut-eye a night.[1]

You probably already have some understanding of the benefits of rest—and the costs of not getting it. Sleep allows us to consolidate and store memories, process emotional experiences, replenish glucose (the molecule that fuels the brain), and clear out beta-amyloid (the waste product that builds up in Alzheimer's patients and disrupts cognitive activity). By contrast, insufficient sleep and fatigue lead to poor judgment, lack of self-control, and impaired creativity. Moreover, there are lesser-known secondary effects in organizations. My research shows that sleep deprivation doesn't just hurt individual performance: When managers lose sleep, their employees' experiences and output are diminished too.

So how can we turn this knowledge into sustained behavior change? A first step for sleep-deprived leaders is to come to terms with just how damaging your fatigue can be—not only to you but also to those who work for you. Next, follow some simple, practical, research-backed advice to ensure that you get better rest, perform to your potential, and bring out the best in the people around you.

Spreading Damage

Historically, scholars have depicted supervision as stable over time—some bosses are just bad, and others aren't. But recent research indicates that individual behavior can vary dramatically from day to day and week to week—and much of this variance can be explained by the quality of a manager's sleep. Indeed, studies have found that when leaders show up for work unrested, they are more likely to lose patience with employees, act in abusive ways, and be seen as less charismatic. There is also a greater likelihood that their subordinates will themselves suffer from sleep deprivation—and even behave unethically.

Idea in Brief

The Problem

You know you should get more sleep. But did you know there is a link between adequate sleep and effective leadership? Most people average only six hours of sleep or less per night, which can lead to poor judgment, lack of self-control, and impaired creativity. The ripple effects of sleep deprivation can result in mistreatment of employees and disengaged, unethical workplaces.

The Solution

You can take steps to improve the quality of your sleep. These include maintaining a regular sleep schedule; avoiding caffeine, nicotine, alcohol, and screen time before bed; tracking your sleep patterns; seeking treatment for sleep disorders; and even incorporating brief naps into your workday.

The Benefits

We know that prioritizing sleep can enhance your own productivity. Well-rested leaders are also better equipped to make sound decisions, exhibit self-control, and foster a positive and ethical work environment. When you sleep well, you'll lead better, and everyone benefits.

In a recent study Cristiano Guarana and I measured the sleep of 40 managers and their 120 direct reports during the first three months of their assigned time working together, along with the quality of these boss-employee relationships.[2] We found that sleep-deprived leaders were more impatient, irritable, and antagonistic, which resulted in worse relationships. We expected that this effect would diminish over time as people got to know each other, but it did not. Sleep deprivation was just as damaging at the end of the three months as it was at the beginning. However, the leaders were completely unaware of the negative dynamic.

Lorenzo Lucianetti, Devasheesh Bhave, Michael Christian, and I found similar results when we asked 88 leaders and their subordinates to complete daily surveys for two weeks: When bosses slept poorly, they were more likely to exhibit abusive behavior the next day, which resulted in lower levels of engagement among subordinates.[3] When the boss doesn't feel rested, the whole unit pays a price.

Sleep also affects managers' ability to inspire and motivate those around them. In a 2016 experiment, Cristiano Guarana, Shazia Nauman, Dejun Tony Kong, and I manipulated the sleep of a sample of students: Some were allowed to get a normal night's worth, while others were randomly assigned to a sleep-deprived condition in which they were awake about two hours longer.[4] We then asked each participant to give a speech on the role of a leader, recorded those talks, and had third parties evaluate the speakers for charisma. Those who were sleep-deprived received scores 13% lower than those in the control group. Why? Previous research has shown that when leaders evince positive emotion, subordinates feel good and therefore perceive the bosses as charismatic. If we don't get enough sleep, we're less likely to feel positive and less able to manage or fake our moods; it's very difficult to pull ourselves out of an insomnia-induced funk.

Furthermore, leaders who discount the value of sleep can negatively impact not just emotions but also behaviors on their teams. Lorenzo Lucianetti, Eli Awtrey, Gretchen Spreitzer, and I conducted a series of studies of what we termed "sleep devaluation"—scenarios in which leaders communicate to subordinates that sleep is unimportant. They may do so by setting an example (for instance, boasting about sleeping only four hours or sending work emails at 3 a.m.), or they may directly shape employees' habits by encouraging people to work during typical sleep hours (perhaps criticizing subordinates for not responding to those 3 a.m. emails, or praising individuals who regularly work late into the night). In our studies, we found that employees pay close attention to such cues and adjust their own behavior accordingly. Specifically, subordinates of leaders who model and encourage poor sleep habits get about 25 fewer minutes of nightly rest than people whose bosses value sleep, and they report that their slumber is lower in quality.

One additional—perhaps more powerful—finding from this research was that leaders' devaluation of sleep may also cause followers to behave less ethically. Bosses who systematically eschewed rest—in comparison to other managers—rated their subordinates as less likely to do the right thing. We suspect this wasn't just a matter of the sleep-deprived leaders' giving tougher ratings; it's likely that employees were actually behaving in less moral ways as a result of the workplace environment or their own sleep deprivation. Indeed, in previous studies we've shown that lack of sleep is directly linked to lapses in ethics.[5]

Overlooked Solutions

Fortunately, there are solutions to help leaders improve the quality and quantity of their sleep. Many of these are well-known but underutilized. They include sticking to a consistent bedtime and wake-up schedule, avoiding certain substances too close to bedtime (caffeine within seven hours, alcohol within three hours, and nicotine within three or four hours), and exercising (but not right before bed). Additionally, relaxation and mindfulness meditation exercises help lower anxiety, making it easier to drift off to sleep.

A new branch of research is beginning to show how important it is to alter smartphone behavior too. Melatonin is a crucial biochemical involved in the process of falling asleep, and light (especially blue light from screens) suppresses its natural production. In research focused on middle managers, Klodiana Lanaj, Russell Johnson, and I found that time spent using smartphones after 9 p.m. came at the expense of sleep, which undermined work engagement the next day.[6] The simple advice is to stop looking at your devices at night. If that's not practical, you might try glasses that filter out blue light. Some researchers have found that these can mitigate the effect on melatonin production, thus helping people fall asleep more easily; I'm now in the very early stages of a study examining how this may improve work outcomes as well.

Savvy leaders are also starting to track their sleep, through either diaries or electronic trackers. But beware: Most sleep trackers have not gone through rigorous validation for accuracy. (Your Fitbit can do many things, but it is not especially good at measuring sleep.) Many phone apps in particular make unsupported claims—for example, that they can track which stage of sleep you're in. However, some devices, such as ActiGraph monitors, are very accurate and can help you determine whether you're overestimating your sleep (we often forget about periods of wakefulness in the night) and whether there are patterns you can change. For example, you might find that although you're in bed for seven hours a night, you're getting only five hours of sleep, fragmented into small segments. Or perhaps you notice that your bedtime drifts later on the weekend, leading to "social jet lag" on Monday, when you have to return to your earlier waking time. With this information, you can make adjustments, such as taking a relaxing bath before bed in hopes of getting more sustained rest, or hitting the sack earlier on Saturday and Sunday nights.

Leaders often overlook two other tools. The first is treatment for sleep disorders. By some estimates, up to 30% of Americans experience insomnia, and more than 5% suffer from sleep apnea. A large majority of people with these issues are never diagnosed or treated. If you are overweight, have a thick neck, snore, and spend adequate time in bed at night but still feel tired, you may have sleep apnea. Partners or spouses are often the first to notice the symptoms, but official diagnoses are typically made after a sleep study that measures oxygen levels and brain waves. You might then be prescribed a continuous positive airway pressure (CPAP) mask to wear at night; by keeping nasal and throat airways open, these devices greatly help sleep apnea patients.

As for insomnia sufferers, they're typically aware of the problem but may not know how to fix it. Jared Miller, Sophie Bostock, and I examined an online program that uses cognitive behavioral therapy to combat this disorder. We found that participants who were randomly assigned to the program experienced improved sleep, more self-control, better moods, and higher job satisfaction, and they became more helpful toward colleagues.[7] The treatment cost only a few hundred dollars per participant, indicating a substantial return on investment. I'm currently in the early stages of another study that will measure the effects of this treatment on leader behaviors and follower outcomes, and I expect similarly beneficial effects.

The other overlooked tool for getting more rest is napping. Too often, leaders view nap breaks as time spent loafing instead of working. However, research clearly indicates that dozing for even 20 minutes can lead to meaningful restoration that improves the quality of work. A brief nap can speed up cognitive processing, decrease errors, and increase stamina for sustained attention to difficult tasks later in the day. One study found that as little as eight minutes of sleep during the day was enough to significantly improve memory.[8]

Many cultures outside the United States have embraced naps as a normal and desirable activity. In Japan, *inemuri*, or napping at work, is typically viewed positively. Midday siestas have long been part of work life in Spain. Now some American leaders are beginning to embrace this form of rest. Tony Hsieh, the CEO of Zappos, is a nap proponent, and organizations such as Google and PriceWaterhouseCoopers have nap pods for employees, understanding that 20 minutes of downtime can make people more effective and productive for many more hours that day.

As a leader, even if you fail to get enough sleep yourself, you should be careful to promote good sleeping behavior. Your employees are watching you for cues about what is important. Avoid bragging about your own lack of sleep, lest you signal to your subordinates that they, too, should deprioritize sleep. If you absolutely must compose an email at 3 a.m., use a delayed-delivery option so that the message isn't sent until 8 a.m. If you must pull an all-nighter on a project, don't hold that up as exemplary behavior.

For pro-sleep role models, look to CEOs such as Ryan Holmes of Hootsuite ("It's not worth depriving yourself of sleep for an extended period of time, no matter how pressing things may seem"); Amazon's Bezos ("Eight hours of sleep makes a big difference for me, and I try hard to make that a priority"); and Huffington, the CEO of Thrive Global, who wrote a whole book on the subject.

It is clear that you can squeeze in more work hours if you sleep less. But remember that the quality of your work—and your leadership—inevitably declines as you do so, often in ways that are invisible to you. As Bezos says, "Making a small number of key decisions well is more important than making a large number of decisions. If you shortchange your sleep, you might get a couple of extra 'productive' hours, but that productivity might be an illusion." Even worse, as my research highlights, you'll negatively affect your subordinates.

If instead you make sleep a priority, you will be a more successful leader who inspires better work in your employees. Don't handicap yourself or your team by failing to get enough rest.

Originally published in September–October 2018. Reprint R1805K

9

Leading in the Flow of Work

by Hitendra Wadhwa

onventional wisdom holds that leadership can be developed through extensive study and training. Many organizations invest a tremendous amount of time and money in programs that teach executives how to influence, inspire, and coach others; build trust; have crucial conversations; give feedback; change people's behavior; and more. Many aspiring leaders comb through books, attend seminars, and seek out mentors, all in an effort to understand leadership's intricate nuances.

My research shows that another approach can complement and accelerate those traditional, competence-focused efforts. It involves tapping into neural pathways in the brain—into faculties everyone already possesses but might not be consistently using at work. Rather than a trait to be acquired, leadership is a state to be activated, my work suggests. And by shifting the emphasis from learning on the sidelines to leading in the moment, executives can achieve real breakthroughs.

This leadership model, which has become the basis for a popular course at Columbia Business School, grew out of work that my consulting firm, Mentora Institute, my team, and I did. In 2006 we began building a repository of more than 1,000 moments of transformative leadership, capturing instances when individuals notably exceeded expectations in critical situations. In 2022, I detailed our insights in a book, *Inner Mastery, Outer Impact,* in which I introduced the main tenets of exemplary leadership and argued that leaders can embody them by tapping into their inner core—the space of highest potential within them, their best self. The presence within us of such a core—of a state of peak performance in which we're calmly aware of our inner and outer conditions and able to adapt our behavior as needed—is being substantiated by scientific studies in a range of fields, including cognitive behavioral therapy, positive psychology, and neuroscience. Yet the idea of it isn't new; across the ages, people have engaged in contemplative practices in an effort to connect with what they have intuited to be their spirit or soul and to express its qualities in their outer pursuits.

My firm has found that executives can tap into their inner core with just 10 to 15 minutes of preparation before a big event. In our research and consulting work, we've validated our approach, which we call *leadership-in-flow.* At SAP, for instance, managers trained in it performed twice as well (at increasing their ratings on leadership trust) as a control group of managers did. And in a cross-organizational study spanning diverse industries, roles, and levels, more than 100 executives who adopted leadership-in-flow saw their ability to achieve successful outcomes—measured by whether they attained their

Idea in Brief

The Opportunity

Conventional leadership development relies heavily on time-consuming study and training. But a new approach, which draws on faculties everyone already possesses, can accelerate and enhance those efforts.

What It Involves

The leadership-in-flow model centers on activating your inner core by tapping into five types of energy: purpose, wisdom, growth, love, and self-realization.

How to Capture It

Using one or more of 25 simple actions, leaders can tailor their responses to evolving situations and unlock peak performance in real time in both themselves and the people they work with.

performance goals—rise by an average of 135% within six weeks. Our findings reveal that people have an innate capacity for exemplary leadership far beyond what many realize.

How exactly do you activate your inner core? In this article, for the first time, I introduce a playbook of quick actions people can use to tap into it and unlock peak performance under real-time pressure—precisely when it matters the most.

Before diving into the specifics, however, let's examine the fundamental shift that leadership-in-flow entails.

A Dynamic State

It's a common organizational practice to evaluate people along a bell curve, rating every individual as a low, average, or high performer. In fact, each of us is the whole bell curve. As a wave of scientific findings shows, the personality and behavior of someone will change with the context that person is in, the thoughts and feelings that individual is experiencing, and who else is present. Someone may be extroverted in one situation, introverted in another; agreeable in one, disagreeable in another. That's why leadership is not a static trait—it is a dynamic state.

But one thing remains constant: When we're "triggered"—emotionally upset—we tend to underperform. Conversely, when we're "centered"—calm, attuned, and open—we're more likely to achieve high performance. This happens when we're connected to our inner core. We transcend ego, attachments, insecurities, impulses, and everyday habits—like interrupting others or appearing agreeable while actually feeling resistant—and act in a way that's best for the cause we're serving.

But a number of things can prevent executives from achieving this state. First, they often walk into pivotal moments feeling stressed—either about other things going on in their lives or about the very situation they're confronting. Second, they simply don't see the greater possibilities their situation offers—to build trust, resolve conflict, inspire a beaten-down team, and so on. Third, once they're in a situation they react in habitual, fixed ways instead of observing the dynamics among people and responding agilely. And last, they focus all their preparation for key events on functional and technical details while paying little to no heed to the human dimension—to adapting themselves to the needs and styles of the people in the room.

Leadership-in-flow is designed to overcome those obstacles. Through it people activate the inner core not just in themselves but also in those they work with, by drawing on energies they already possess.

The Core Energies

Our leadership model, which builds on both ancient wisdom and contemporary science, focuses on five types of energy:

- *Purpose* (committed to a noble cause)

- *Wisdom* (calm and receptive to the truth)

- *Growth* (curious and open to learning)

- *Love* (connected with those you work with and serve)

- *Self-realization* (centered in a joyful spirit)

Across all the exemplary leadership moments we studied, people consistently used a small set of actions to tap into one or more of these five energies. The actions were swift and straightforward, often taking just seconds. Our analysis revealed that 25 actions—four to seven for each type of energy—showed up regularly. (I'll describe some of them in the examples that follow, but you can find a complete list in the sidebar "How to Achieve Leadership-in-Flow.")

By taking these actions, leaders can break free from rigid behavioral scripts. One profound moment in the history of the Cold War illustrates how.

On December 16, 1984, British prime minister Margaret Thatcher hosted Mikhail Gorbachev, a member of the Soviet Politburo who was seen as a potential future leader of the country, at what ended up being a five-hour lunch at Chequers, the prime minister's country home. Thatcher wasted no time in firing the first salvo, stating, "I want there to be no misunderstanding between us. . . I hate communism."

"Very quickly, the argument between Margaret and me became very heated," Gorbachev later recalled, according to Jonathan

Aitken's book *Margaret Thatcher: Power and Personality*. "She was accusing the Soviet Union of all sorts of unfair things. I did not accuse Britain of anything." The two turned their backs to each other in the middle of lunch, and Gorbachev's wife, Raisa, stunned by Thatcher's attack, indicated to her husband, "It's over!" For a moment Gorbachev thought they should leave.

And then something remarkable happened. Gorbachev centered himself and considered his intentions in meeting Thatcher. "We are guests here; the conversation must continue," he thought. He reframed the situation in his mind from "She's attacking my government!" to "She's promoting her principles."

"Mrs. Thatcher," Gorbachev said. "I know you are a person with an acute mind and high personal principles. Please bear in mind that I am the same kind of person." She responded with a nod. He then continued, "Let me assure you that I have not come here with instructions from the Politburo to persuade you to become a member of the Communist Party." Thatcher burst into laughter. "The tension was broken," recalled Gorbachev, "and the discussion continued, although it soon [heated] up again but in better ways."

The meeting proved to be a turning point in the Cold War. It convinced Thatcher—and subsequently, the U.S. president Ronald Reagan—that Gorbachev, in contrast to past Soviet leaders, was a man they could work with. "I actually rather liked him," Thatcher later told Reagan.

Gorbachev himself reflected, "It was then, during that talk in Chequers, that the special relationship was born . . . We worked closely and fruitfully together to advance the important processes of that time—curbing the arms race, European developments, German unification, and reversing Iraq's aggression in the Middle East."

How to Achieve Leadership-in-Flow

Leadership is not a set of traits to be learned; it is a state that can be attained by establishing a positive intention and then activating five core energies we all possess via quick actions that take just a few seconds to execute. Below are 25 actions that you can use to tap your core energies.

Purpose Energy: Committed to a Noble Cause

1. *Appeal to values and purpose.* Discover and understand people's dearly held values and purpose and then tie them to what you're seeking.

2. *Reaffirm and reexpress.* When facing an unexpected change or a setback, find a way to reapply your core values and purpose to the new situation.

3. *Embark on a hero's journey.* Craft a compelling vision that inspires people to pursue a goal despite tough challenges.

4. *Push, pull, pause, pivot.* When you run into resistance, find a way to move forward by refining your idea and then presenting it again, shelving it if the costs are too high, waiting for changes that might renew interest in it, or reimagining it altogether.

Wisdom Energy: Calm and Receptive to the Truth

5. *Understand before you act.* Approach an issue with heightened curiosity, and fully explore it before making your move.

6. *Disarm.* When you encounter disagreement, find something true in what the other party is saying and affirm it.

(continued)

How to Achieve Leadership-in-Flow *(continued)*

7. *Fuse opposing viewpoints.* Find a way to integrate contradictory positions into a more nuanced and balanced perspective. For instance, if team members disagree about the quality of their presentation, their manager might point out that while the presentation was analytically persuasive, it overlooked building an emotional connection.

8. *Dial an emotion up or down.* Intensify positive feelings or dampen negative ones to bring out the best in yourself and others. Sensing rising frustration in a team meeting, a manager can shift the conversation to past successes and team strengths before turning people's attention back to the debate.

9. *Direct emotional energy.* Harness the energy your feelings are producing to advance your purpose. For instance, use the pain of defeat to motivate a team to practice with greater discipline.

10. *Untwist your thinking.* Eliminate distorted thoughts so that you can see the situation in a clear, objective light. No, a presentation wasn't a "total disaster."

11. *Create the right frame.* Describe challenges, opportunities, and assignments in a way that brings out the best in people.

Growth Energy: Curious and Open to Learning

12. *Practice a growth mindset.* Recognize the vast untapped potential that exists in you and others.

13. *Solicit advice.* Gain a deeper understanding of others' perspectives by asking experts and stakeholders to openly share their thoughts.

14. *Acknowledge, apologize, address.* Swiftly acknowledge, apologize for, and correct mistakes.

15. *Learn from adversity.* Use setbacks and failures to help you and others become better—not bitter.

16. *Anticipate, assess, adjust.* Think about the challenges that may lie ahead and plan how you will evaluate and adapt to them.

Love Energy: Connected with Those You Work with and Serve

17. *Appreciate.* Recognize positive qualities in situations and people.

18. *Affiliate.* Find common ground with others.

19. *Deepen human connection.* Create strong emotional bonds with others by accepting and offering bids for connection.

20. *Empathize.* Attune yourself, without judgment, to the emotions and thoughts of others and make them feel understood.

21. *Act/express thoughtfully.* Bring a deep sense of caring to how you make tough decisions and communicate hard truths.

Self-Realization Energy: Centered in a Joyful Spirit

22. *Get centered.* Step back from your thoughts and feelings and focus on the tranquility deep inside you.

23. *Affirm a core identity.* Help people see a positive quality as already being present at their core. For example, a manager might say, "Remember how composed you were at your last presentation? That is an intrinsic quality I've seen you possess. Tap into it, and this meeting will go smoothly."

24. *Cultivate intuition.* Generate creative insights on critical issues by inducing a relaxed state of mind, for example, by taking a walk or meditating.

25. *Spark joy.* Cheer others up with small uplifting acts.

Was Gorbachev in that pivotal moment of impasse at lunch having a crucial conversation with Thatcher? Influencing her? Inspiring her? Giving feedback? Building trust? Changing her behavior? He was quite evidently engaging in all those traditional leadership activities. Yet in that moment, he was focused on one thing—activating the inner core in himself and in Thatcher. He did so with a few simple actions.

First, he established a positive intention and tapped into purpose by *reaffirming and reexpressing* his reasons for meeting with Thatcher and deciding to stay and reengage with her. Second, he showed wisdom by *creating the right frame*—by looking at the situation more constructively. Third, he evoked love by *showing appreciation* for her acute mind and her high personal principles and *establishing an affiliation* with her—stating that he was the same kind of person. Last, instead of criticizing her for trying to convert him, he showed her how amusing it would be to her if he were trying to convert her, *sparking joy* (self-realization). Those actions instantly changed the tone of the meeting and helped him switch his leadership style from arguing to bridging.

Like Gorbachev, we all have more than one style. By drawing on our core energies, we can pull away from a limiting identification with any particular style and adapt to the present moment. It is worth noting, however, that leadership-in-flow does not work by faking it. If Gorbachev hadn't first truly felt admiration for Thatcher's acute mind and her principles, Thatcher probably would have sensed from his demeanor that he wasn't being genuine and would have responded much more coolly.

Most of us already have experience with the actions that activate the core energies. We all, for instance, show appreciation and build affiliations in everyday life (though it might not occur to many of us to use these actions if we were in Gorbachev's situation). The neural pathways for these actions are present in most people's brains. Since it's much easier to activate existing pathways than to build pathways from scratch, leadership-in-flow is accessible to everyone—people in all roles and at all levels.

Moreover, as Gorbachev's story shows, the energies and actions can be harnessed to advance traditional leadership skills. Because they're like a standardized set of building blocks, their use can help radically simplify competence-focused training.

Getting into the Flow

When great athletes are in a flow state, their achievements look effortless—yet of course everything in their daily routines (from training to warm-ups to postmatch analyses) is intentional. The same is true with leadership. Indeed, in emphasizing leadership in the moment, I don't want to minimize the importance of crafting a planned approach beforehand (to increase the chances of reaching the right state) and afterward (to learn from the experience and improve).

I advise executives to begin by targeting a specific upcoming event, like a board presentation or a negotiation, and homing in on a single objective, whether it's building urgency, gaining buy-in, resolving conflict, or inspiring peak performance. Having no concrete goal or juggling too many goals can hinder a flow state. Executives should then replace any negative emotions or beliefs about that situation with a positive intention. If, for example, you are feeling unmotivated about a proposal-review meeting with your CFO because you believe she's already decided against funding your request, you could set your intention to be "I will draw out my CFO's perspective and points of resistance, build greater understanding between us, and prepare the conditions for a strong long-term partnership with her."

Research shows that our intentions influence our emotions, thoughts, and perceptions, and that those in turn influence our behavior. When you believe other participants in a meeting won't respect your perspective, or that a subordinate won't be happy with your feedback, or that one party will have to lose for the other to win, you'll be less likely to engage in behaviors that build trust, open people's minds, and deepen understanding.

Next, I tell executives to pick three to five actions they can take to advance their goal for the event. They should base their choices on the energies they're most drawn to and the context they're in. To resolve a conflict, for example, they may activate wisdom by *fusing opposing viewpoints*, or they may activate love by *empathizing* and affiliating. Leadership-in-flow does not require a fixed sequence of actions in any situation; executives should pick suitable actions that feel authentic to them.

Consider how Adrian, a physician, resolved a disruptive situation that occurred at his hospital when the administration suddenly mandated a daily morning huddle for clinicians and staff without consulting them. The clinicians and staff were deeply upset because the huddle was held during patient appointment hours, and they felt it would negatively affect patient care. As a member of the operations committee, Adrian decided to intervene. He asked the administration to put the program on hold for a week. He began with an action that activates wisdom: *understand before you act*. By holding conversations with administrators about their motivations and with clinicians and staff about the complications they were experiencing, he discovered that top hospital systems had implemented similar huddles and found they greatly improved communication and workflow and created a sense of community. He then convened a meeting of the clinicians and staff. He set the tone by expressing appreciation (thereby creating love energy) for the tremendous sacrifices people were making. He then drew on purpose by *appealing to the values and purpose* of those present by reminding them of their collective commitment to providing the best patient care. Next he took two more actions that lead to wisdom: He created the right frame by helping people switch from an "us versus them" attitude to jointly looking for the best path forward, and he fused opposing points of view by getting the two sides to see the value of not just doing their work well but also coming together to share, learn, and connect. It worked. "I received several text messages and emails," he recounts, "acknowledging how I had been able to turn around the situation and bridge the divide."

Once executives have chosen the actions they'll undertake, they should spend five to 10 minutes before the event reviewing them and the intention they have set and taking time to *center themselves*. (There are any number of practices people can use to do this, such as deep breathing or a brief meditation.) As part of this they should spend two minutes visualizing how they'll perform each chosen action. Our data shows that people who engage in such visualizations are 70% more likely to succeed at their goals. "It's like the warm-up that athletes do before a game to perform better and avoid injury," a key account director at IBM told us. "We executives too need to warm up our minds prior to events to think better and to prevent meetings from going in the wrong direction."

Such preparation also frees up more of the brain's executive system—the frontal lobes—to deal with evolving dynamics, allowing people to adapt quickly as conditions change. They can use whatever action makes the most sense to them, moment by moment, shifting toward different energies as the event unfolds.

At one financial services company, tensions were running high on the analytics team of an executive called Roger. It was getting a lot of assignments but didn't have a good process for prioritizing them. Deadlines were being missed, and teammates were blaming one another, much to Roger's irritation. He decided to bring the team together for a conversation. To put aside his negative emotions, he set the intention: "I will create positive energy and rally the team around my vision." He started the meeting by showing empathy and appreciation. "I understand how difficult it has been these last few weeks," he said. "I recognize how hard you all have been working, despite these obstacles." The love energy these actions released helped put his team at ease. Sensing an opening, he switched to activating growth energy by *soliciting advice*, inviting the team members to share their perspectives on the challenges they faced. Seeing that some were nervous, he gently nudged them and thoughtfully probed. As team members got more comfortable sharing their perspectives, one suggested that they start saying no to new requests, while another pushed back because that would compromise their objective of being a responsive team. Roger fused these opposing viewpoints by proposing that they become better at setting and resetting expectations about deliverables and deadlines with their internal clients. "Every person in the room felt personally accountable, engaged, and invested," he recalls. As a result, valuable ideas emerged about how the team should prioritize work, and the chronic delays were alleviated.

Sometime after an event, executives should do a postmortem to assess how well it went, how successful they were at meeting their goals and using the chosen actions, and what they learned from it. Even when things don't turn out as desired, this practice can produce valuable insights. As a vice president of business development at Wilton Re told us, postmortems have helped him "translate instances of 'failure' into opportunities for growth," allowing him to find pride in moments when he honored his intention and tied it to his values.

Building Success upon Success

In our cross-organizational study, we saw that the performance of the more than 100 executives who were practicing leadership-in-flow for six weeks kept improving from one event to the next. As I've noted, by the end their ability to achieve their goals had more than doubled on average, even though the objectives, context, and other parties involved in each event differed. We believe this is because of the consistency of the building blocks— the five core energies and 25 actions. As executives become more experienced at using them, they can effectively apply them in a wide variety of situations.

These findings align with research on expert performance showing that experts are more effective at organizing information— something psychologists call "chunking"—in their disciplines than novices are. Experts recognize structures that novices do not, are able to both take a high-level view and observe detailed nuances in a situation, and can transfer their chunking strategies more effortlessly to new contexts. Similarly, our research shows that executives who are experienced with leadership-in-flow can tune in to the energies in the room while others may only see outer behaviors; can see situations both from the high-level, five-energy perspective and from the more-nuanced actions perspective; and can transfer their ability to harness the core energies from one context to another.

Robin, a senior manager at a professional services firm, was assigned by her employer to take on a challenging client project in which multiple deliverables were due under a tight deadline. In preparing for her first meeting with the clients, Robin decided to focus on activating wisdom by creating the right frame and love by *acting/expressing thoughtfully* (bringing a deep sense of caring to how you make tough decisions and communicate hard truths). Though she had received training on acting/expressing thoughtfully, she learned about creating the right frame in the midst of her preparation, when reviewing the 25 actions.

"The meeting got off to a surprisingly rocky start," Robin later recalled. "The clients started to give negative feedback on another project, and that threatened to derail the conversation." Robin's normal response to such criticism would have been to defend her organization's work and to engage in problem-solving on the issues raised. Instead, she decided in real time to draw on wisdom by *disarming* (finding something true in what an opposing party is saying and affirming it), an action she had used in earlier contexts, by agreeing with the clients that their concerns were important and assuring them that her team would look into them. Seeing the clients calm down, she brought them back to the purpose of their meeting, emphasizing how crucial it was to give full attention to the issues they needed to resolve. She positioned it as an opportunity for the two teams to hammer out details now to avoid problems later. She was able to get the meeting back on track and to get agreement on what her team and the clients would do to complete the project successfully.

Leadership-in-flow makes it easy for executives to expand their arsenal of actions over time, as Robin did. Our analysis has revealed that once they start practicing leadership-in-flow, executives perform just as well with actions they've picked up during event preparation as they do with actions they've been trained on at a workshop. This is because the actions are simple, and the neural pathways needed to use most of them are already present in us.

. . .

In our early years, we associate learning with structured classrooms and set curriculums. Yet as we navigate the complexities of work and life, it becomes evident that some of our most profound breakthroughs emerge when we are "in the flow"—when we immerse ourselves in real-world experiences and challenges, respond in real time as conditions change, and tap into virtues and energies already present in our core.

Losing touch with the five energies amid life's whirlwind is natural, but rekindling them is within our reach. All we need to do is focus on a goal, open our hearts and minds to new possibilities, and select the right actions that will activate our inner core—a state from which remarkable performance arises.

Originally published in January–February 2024. Reprint S24011

When Your High Standards Derail Your Success

by Anne Sugar and Karen Walker

No one would argue that having high standards for your work and your team is a bad thing. Yet sometimes, extraordinarily high standards can be unproductive and halt forward movement in your leadership career.

Leadership can be messy. Things often don't go as planned. Rather than accepting this as a natural part of life, if your standards are too inflexible, you'll feel perpetually frustrated because neither you nor your team live up to your goals.

In practice, this can look like:

- You and your team don't seem to be on the same page in meetings.

- Projects never get completed in the timeline you set forth.

- Your manager says, "Eighty percent done is good enough," yet you delay getting work to them until it's "perfect."

- You and your team always work long hours.

- Your team is showing signs of burnout (and so are you).

It may feel personally satisfying to see a project completed at your perception of "100%." But at what cost? And what is the long-term net good? It might be less than you think, both for the company and for you. All this extra energy is exhausted seeking perfection when it could be used to innovate or take a new step in your career. Your high standards can become a detriment, inhibiting good work and sabotaging your career.

If this sounds like you, here are four ideas to help you adjust your expectations and get you moving forward again.

Pause

Instead of charging ahead, take a beat. Set aside 15 to 30 minutes in your week to ask yourself the following questions:

- How long have I had these standards in place?

- Are they in line with the company's goals and needs?

- When did I last consider how I'm measuring success for the current situation? Do I need to recalibrate?

- Have I ever discussed these standards with my team? (It's not uncommon for leaders to have incredibly high standards that they've never communicated.)

- What has worked with these standards in place?

- Why did I set these standards?

The Problem

It's a good thing to have high standards, right? No one would argue that it's bad to want the best for you and your team, but holding yourself and others to measures that are inflexible is unsustainable and may become counterproductive. This rigidity can hinder progress, strain relationships, and even jeopardize career advancement.

The Solution

Consider whether your expectations may be too extreme by pausing to reflect on whether your standards are realistic, learning when to be flexible, evaluating whether your standards fit within your organizational culture, and finding more-balanced solutions by engaging in productive conflict.

The Benefits

You can set and maintain high standards without letting them become a barrier to success or earning yourself a reputation as a micromanager or rigid thinker. Taking the time to align your standards with your team and company culture, goals, and values will foster a more adaptable and collaborative work environment.

- What do other people on my team think about these standards?
- Has the culture shifted? Should my goals shift?

Then, consider this question: What does "good enough" look like for you?

Karen often sees this scenario in high-growth companies: The "best" way of accomplishing tasks gets in the way of "good enough" for the time and budget available. Be clear about your organization's priorities. Assess where you are, what needs to be adjusted, and how you need to communicate with stakeholders. Sometimes good is good enough.

Know When to Be Flexible

High standards can't be reached without other people on board. Do others understand your vision? Ask yourself these questions:

- How much social capital do I have with this team?

- How does the room respond when I deliver feedback?

- Are my standards making a meaningful difference in whether we accomplish our goals?

One of Anne's clients with exacting standards regularly made her team members stay until midnight to make minor changes to proposals. Her team was losing motivation fast. Through coaching, the client determined the extra hours were not worth it; she needed to flex her standards so that she wouldn't burn out her team. The incremental improvements resulting from those extra hours weren't helping the bottom line. This client derived greater benefit from letting the team go home after normal working hours. The product didn't suffer, and the team didn't feel resentful.

Another one of Anne's clients had a disconnect with his team. He thought he'd been clear on his vision for the department. However, vision-sharing is not "one and done"; leaders need to continually share their vision with team members and get everyone's buy-in. Because the team lacked clarity, they weren't aligned on work standards and what would be "good enough." Once the leader sat down and shared his vision again, team members got it—and the work improved.

Consider Your Culture Fit

You may need to zoom out and look at the bigger picture. Ask yourself whether you're in the right company or department to leverage your skills. There's no such thing as a perfect job or a perfect company, but you may be better suited to another environment. Ask yourself:

- What am I hearing in my performance reviews?

- What do the outputs from my 360s look like?

- What is the culture of the company? How do I fit within it?

- Is leadership supportive of my work? (Ask your manager for candid feedback.)

- Am I working on the company's highest priorities?

Check-ins like this are also not a "one and done"; you'll need to do them continually throughout your career.

Karen will often provide 360 assessments for her clients. They are all individual high performers, but not all have high-performing *team* skills. For some clients, the gap in team skills is a major oversight. If you feel you aren't being as effective in team settings as you'd like, ask for feedback. Then, listen and learn from what you receive. What you perceive as the right way to do something may be only the right way for *you* to do it. Or maybe you've been successful with this method in the past with another team—but *this* team, these specific people, work differently. To be effective, you need to work differently, too.

Engage in Productive Conflict

Your team members, peers, and managers may not understand the importance of your high standards and may be confused by your lack of flexibility when conflicts arise. Just because someone disagrees doesn't mean you need to compete—or shut down and walk away from the project or conversation. Engage in productive, respectful conflict and seek common ground with your colleagues. Remember that you don't need to win every disagreement. Pause, allow space for the other person, and take your time in reaching a resolution. Approach the conflict assuming your colleagues' good intent and desire to see the work done well.

. . .

It can be frustrating to have high standards that are not valued. Consider: Do you need to be more flexible, or should you move to a company more aligned with your exacting standards? Either way, don't let your standards halt your career trajectory.

Adapted from hbr.org, November 25, 2024. Reprint H08HSV

10

Use Strategic Thinking to Create the Life You Want

by Rainer Strack, Susanne Dyrchs, and Allison Bailey

n times of crisis, many of us ponder existential questions about health, security, purpose, career, family, and legacy. However, more often than not, such contemplation is short-lived. The demands of everyday life—the here and now—can overwhelm us, leaving little time to think about the long term and what we are working toward. As a result, when faced with life decisions both big and small, we are left with nothing to guide us but emotion or intuition.

The corporate equivalent, of course, is attempting to run a business without a strategy, which every HBR reader knows is a losing proposition. But as longtime consultants to organizations around the world, we wondered: Could we adapt the model for strategic thinking that we use with institutional clients to help individuals design better futures for themselves? The answer is yes, and the result is a program that we call Strategize Your Life.

We've tested it with more than 500 people—including students, young professionals, middle-aged employees and managers, C-suite executives, board members, and retirees—to help them develop their individual life strategies.

You can create a life strategy at any time, but it can feel especially appropriate at certain milestones—graduating from school, starting your first job, being promoted, becoming an empty-nester, retiring—or after a major life event, such as a health scare, a divorce, the loss of a job, a midlife crisis, or the death of a loved one. When you have a strategy, you will be better able to navigate all those transitions and difficult moments, building resilience and finding more joy and fulfilment while minimizing stress. This article will help you get started.

A Surprising Symmetry

Every corporate strategy project is different. But the hundreds that we've conducted for large organizations have had commonalities, including the use of certain methodologies and tools. We typically work through seven steps, each guided by a question (see the exhibit "From corporate strategy to life strategy"):

1. How does the organization define success?

2. What is our purpose?

3. What is our vision?

4. How do we assess our business portfolio?

5. What can we learn from benchmarks?

6. What portfolio choices can we make?

7. How can we ensure a successful, sustained change?

Idea in Brief

The Problem

Sometimes juggling the demands of everyday life can be overwhelming, leaving you little time to think deeply about a long-term vision for your life. What are you ultimately working toward? Without a plan to guide you, you're left to make large and small life decisions based on emotion or intuition.

The Solution

A 2 × 2, of course! You can adapt the strategic thinking you use to excel at work to plan your life. Reflect on and answer seven key questions to define success, purpose, and vision, and assess your life portfolio. This process will help you identify areas for improvement and set actionable objectives.

The Benefits

You are the best person to decide and define your purpose and create the vision for what will make a great life for you. This approach can help you navigate difficult situations and major life transitions with more resilience and joy. Creating a clear strategy can help you make informed decisions that align with your long-term goals and values and build a fulfilling career and life.

These steps can be easily adapted to an individual:

1. How do I define a great life?

2. What is my life purpose?

3. What is my life vision?

4. How do I assess my life portfolio?

5. What can I learn from benchmarks?

6. What portfolio choices can I make?

7. How can I ensure a successful, sustained life change?

From corporate strategy to life strategy

The questions that organizations use to set a course for the future can be easily adapted to help individuals do the same.

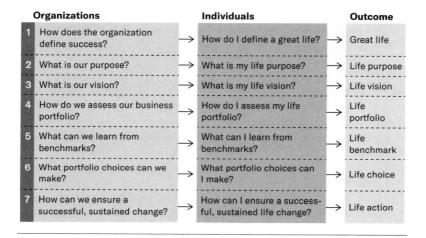

	Organizations	Individuals	Outcome
1	How does the organization define success?	→ How do I define a great life? →	Great life
2	What is our purpose?	→ What is my life purpose? →	Life purpose
3	What is our vision?	→ What is my life vision? →	Life vision
4	How do we assess our business portfolio?	→ How do I assess my life portfolio? →	Life portfolio
5	What can we learn from benchmarks?	→ What can I learn from benchmarks? →	Life benchmark
6	What portfolio choices can we make?	→ What portfolio choices can I make? →	Life choice
7	How can we ensure a successful, sustained change?	→ How can I ensure a successful, sustained life change? →	Life action

As the former head of strategy for a U.S.-based *Fortune* 50 company told us, "Knowing the right questions is much harder than having the answers." Just as corporate strategy is an integrated set of choices that positions a company to win, life strategy is an integrated set of choices that positions a person to live a great life. What's more, we can apply tools from classic organizational strategy and other realms to help you find answers to the seven questions above and make better decisions.

Critics might say that you can't transfer concepts from business to life. In the 1960s there were similar concerns about whether strategy ideas from the military and politics could apply to the corporate world. The management guru Peter Drucker even changed the title of his 1964 book from *Business Strategy* to *Managing for Results* because everyone he and his publisher asked told them that strategy belonged to those realms, not to business. Yet we've also seen business-world principles employed to improve people's self-management. For example, in their best-selling book *Designing Your Life*, Stanford University's Bill Burnett and Dave Evans modified the design thinking they used in software development to help individuals.

Strategize Your Life is our attempt to do the same for strategic thinking in a concrete, step-by-step way. We believe it can lead you to new insights on how you define and find your great life. Our goal is to give your emotion and intuition an analytical partner.

In surveying our workshop and coaching session participants, we found that, in the past, only 21% had outlined what a great life means to them, 9% had identified their purpose, 12% had set a vision for their life, 17% had created concrete goals and milestones, and a paltry 3% had developed what could be called a life strategy. These are critically important issues that very few of us are spending enough time on.

As Martha, a 26-year-old graduate student, explains, "Life keeps taking shape. . . . When all the Christmas parties and weddings and trips are suddenly over, you ask yourself, Have I really lived or has life just happened to me?" She was eager to be more proactive. "What better help is there than a high-level plan for life?" she asks. "Not to strictly follow it and forbid life to unfold, but to have a common thread. What should my story be? What should I have experienced so that in the end I can say to myself, 'I have lived'?"

Unlike most self-help books, we don't present one golden path to happiness or life satisfaction. Because everyone is unique, we give you the tools to find your own path in a seven-step life strategy process. In step 1 you define what a great life means for you. In step 2 you outline your purpose; in step 3 your life vision.

Step 4 is a portfolio analysis of how you spend your 168-hour week, while step 5 involves setting life satisfaction benchmarks. In step 6 you incorporate the results of the first five steps and determine your choices and potential changes in your life, and in step 7 you map out a plan for putting your choices into action. We recommend that you take notes throughout so that, by the end, you can put an initial version of your life strategy on a single page. (To help, we created a life strategy worksheet, which you can access using the QR code near the end of the chapter and you should fill out after you've gone through all the steps.)

This work may seem daunting, but in practice it should take you only a few hours. That said, it might not be easy. You will have to challenge yourself and go beyond the obvious. But you shouldn't give up, because the answers you'll discover are so worthwhile. After all, what's more important than your life? Commit to thinking strategically about it, look forward to the insights you will gain, and enjoy the journey.

The Seven Steps

The process begins with a simple yet profound question:

1. How do I define a great life?

The starting point of any corporate strategy process is to define fundamental metrics for success. For instance, does the organization want its strategy to focus on driving sales, shareholder value, or positive societal impact?

What are the right metrics in an individual's life? Our social norms and hierarchies might suggest we measure ourselves with money, fame, and power. But studies have shown that money leads to greater happiness only to the extent that our basic needs are met, after which its returns diminish or even plateau. Other research shows many of us are on a "hedonic treadmill": After we get a pay raise, are promoted, or purchase something that triggers a pleasurable high, we return to our original level of happiness. And then there is social comparison—no matter what you achieve, someone will always be richer, more famous, or more powerful than you.

The ancient Greeks saw two main dimensions of a great life: *hedonia* (a focus on pleasure) and *eudaimonia* (a focus on virtues and on meaning). More recently, scholars have pointed to the importance of social connection. A study of more than 27,000 people in Asia found a strong correlation between being married and being satisfied with life, while a study that has followed 268 Harvard College men from 1938 to the present, and was expanded to include their children and wives, as well as a study that has followed 456 residents of inner-city Boston since the 1970s, also expanded to include children and wives, found that meaningful relationships were the key driver of long-term happiness. The late Harvard Business School professor Clayton Christensen agreed: In his classic HBR article "How Will You Measure Your Life?" he wrote, "I've concluded that the metric by which God will assess my life isn't dollars but the individual people whose lives I've touched."

A framework that includes all these factors—hedonic, eudemonic, and relational—is the PERMA model, introduced by Martin Seligman, the founder of positive psychology and a University of Pennsylvania professor, in his 2011 book *Flourish*. Other researchers later developed it into PERMA-V, which stands for Positive emotions (frequent feelings of pleasure and contentment), Engagement (being in the flow, losing track of time), Relationships (mutual feelings of caring, support, and love), Meaning (contributing to making the world a better place), Achievement (striving for success or mastery, reaching goals), and Vitality (being healthy and energetic).

To determine what makes a great life for you, start with each element in PERMA-V, or even add your own categories, such as autonomy or spirituality. Then rate each one's importance to you on a scale from 0 (not important) to 10 (very important). Try to recall periods of deep satisfaction in your past and consider what triggered them.

In the first step of strategy projects, we conduct a comprehensive analysis of the status quo. So, you should also rate your current satisfaction with each dimension on a scale from 0 (not at all satisfied) to 10 (very satisfied). This quick assessment will give you a rough idea of how you define a great life and initial ideas about what you need to change.

2. What is my life purpose?

For a corporate strategy to be successful, it must be anchored to the organization's purpose, which lies at the intersection of these two questions: (1) What are we good at? and (2) What does the world need? It also must take into account: What are our values? What excites us? Using these questions, we've helped companies around the world develop purpose statements. A purpose statement serves as an important guardrail for your strategy and is a North Star for your organization.

The same questions can be used to find your life purpose. Ask yourself, What am I good at? Think about situations at work or in other areas of life in which you have demonstrated critical strengths such as creativity, teamwork, or communication. Then ask yourself, What are my core values? Think about critical decisions you've made and principles you hold dear that have provided direction, such as honesty, fairness, or integrity. There are dozens of online lists and tests to help you consider your most important values. The next question is, Which activities light me up? Perhaps your answers include mentoring, problem-solving, or engaging with different types of people. Finally, ask yourself, What need can I help address in the world? It could be one of the 17 Sustainable Development Goals of the United Nations, such as health, education, gender equality, or climate action, or it could be something much more general, such as love, kindness, trust, or security.

In the purpose-defining stage of strategy projects, we conduct belief audits to get input from many stakeholders. Do the same. Ask friends or family members what your strengths are, what values you live by, what things excite you, and what need you might help fill.

Draw from your own answers and theirs to draft a purpose statement, and then ask for feedback on it. Or you can engage ChatGPT in an interactive dance, using the answers to the four questions as input to help you develop your purpose statement, as Tom, a climate physicist, did in one of our recent workshops.

When Joudi, a Kurdish refugee from Syria currently living in Germany, went through this exercise, he identified his core strengths as ambition, passion, and hunger for knowledge. His core values were justice, peace, family, and charity. He said he was most excited by innovation, neurosurgery, and entrepreneurship (notably his experiences selling accessories as a street vendor in Istanbul and founding a multilingual AI-powered integration support platform for Ukrainians who had fled their country for Germany). As for the world needs he wanted to address, Joudi cited healthcare, freedom, and equality. In the end, he wrote this purpose statement: "Remain medically passionate, willing to learn, entrepreneurial, and strong-willed to drive medical innovation and create equitable access to healthcare for people."

A chief human resources officer at a global industrial company wanted to step down from her current role but was unsure whether she should look for a similar role in another company or do something completely different. She went through the seven steps and came up with a simple purpose statement, "To help and lead others to aspire," through which she realized that she did want another senior HR role, just in a different company.

There are other methods for defining one's life purpose, of course. But it's important to find the time and a way to do it. We've seen some workshop participants sharpen their existing purpose ideas, while others have had a real aha moment, finally understanding what they were meant to do. Purpose guides your life strategy.

3. What is my life vision?

The next step in building a corporate strategy is to set out a vision for the future. We typically ask leadership teams where they want their organization to be—in terms of innovation, growth, product portfolio, market presence, and so forth—in five to 10 years. Often we have them ask themselves questions like, What newspaper headline about our company would we like to read a decade from now?

Individuals should also strive to envision who they want to become in the years ahead. As the Stoic philosopher Seneca said, "If you do not know which port you are sailing to, no wind is favorable." At the same time, you want to remain open to surprises and serendipity. Seneca commented on this as well: "Luck is what happens when preparation meets opportunity." Strategizing your life is the preparation.

So, ask yourself: What story would I like people to tell about me five to 10 years from now? What would I do if money wasn't an issue? What will the 80-year-old me not want to have missed in life? Your purpose and your strengths might also trigger some ideas about your vision.

For this step we have used a photo-sorting exercise similar to what our corporate clients use in branding and innovation strategy projects. Out of 180 photos, workshop participants select two to four that best represent their personal and professional vision—what one person described as a "mood board."

In both business and individual life strategy, a vision can give you focus. Jim, who will soon be a doctor, had a purpose statement that was rather general: "Bring people together and share passions." His vision was more concrete and specific: "To create spaces for more social encounters, such as a medical practice with a shared coffee shop, and to get involved in homeless medicine." Your vision should be equally descriptive.

You might end up with a short list of bullet points or a one-sentence summary of your vision. No matter how you capture it, a vision statement can be powerful in guiding your life. An example we love comes from our colleague Sebastian when he was 14. After a poor math test result, his teacher told him, "Teaching you is a waste of time," and warned he'd never get a high school diploma. For the next couple of years Sebastian took that to heart, skipped school, and started working as a bricklayer. Eventually, however, he decided to make a change, and it began with this vision statement: "I will go to university and get a PhD and then go back to my math teacher—all in the next

10 years." He did just that, graduating summa cum laude with a PhD in economics, and in another 10 years he was a managing director and a partner at BCG.

4. How do I assess my life portfolio?

Companies typically use portfolio analysis to assess their business units on key parameters such as market growth or share and to decide where to invest capital. BCG is well known for its 2×2 growth-share matrix.

But what is the equivalent of a business unit in life? We focus on six strategic life areas (SLAs): relationships; body, mind, and spirituality; community and society; job, learning, and finances; interests and entertainment; and personal care. We then subdivide the six SLAs into 16 strategic life units (SLUs). (For a full list of the SLUs, see the exhibit "The key areas of life.")

And what are the equivalents of capital expenditures in life? Time, energy, and money. A week has 168 hours. How do you spend them? Being with your significant other or family, working, playing sports, attending church, getting a good night's rest?

Look back at the past year, including holidays, and assess how much time you spent on each of the 16 SLUs in an average week. When an activity crosses categories, split the time between them. For example, if you went jogging with your significant other for one hour a week, allocate half an hour to the significant other SLU and half an hour to the physical health/sports SLU. Next, rate all 16 SLUs on a scale of 0 to 10 based on how important they are to you. Then rate the satisfaction you derive from each on the same scale. (This goes one level deeper than the similar PERMA-V exercise.)

Now sketch out your own 2×2; we call it the Strategic Life Portfolio (see an example in the exhibit "A sample strategic life

The key areas of life

People spend their time, energy, and money in six strategic life areas, which can be subdivided into 16 strategic life units. Think about how much time you currently spend on each and rank both its importance and the satisfaction it gives you using a 0–10 scale.

Strategic life areas	Strategic life units	Descriptions
1. Relationships	Significant other	Time with partner, dates
	Family	Engaging with kids, parents, siblings
	Friendship	Time with friends
2. Body, mind, and spirituality	Physical health/sports	Exercise, physical therapy
	Mental health/mindfulness	Psychotherapy, meditation
	Spirituality/faith	Religious practice
3. Community and society	Community/citizenship	Membership in local clubs, jury duty
	Societal engagement	Volunteering, activism
4. Job, learning, and finances	Job/career	Work
	Education/learning	Classes, training
	Finances	Planning, investing
5. Interests and entertainment	Hobbies/interests	Reading, collectibles
	Online entertainment	Social media, TV, gaming
	Offline entertainment	Vacations, theater, sporting events
6. Personal care	Physiological needs	Eating, sleeping
	Activities of daily living	Commuting, housework

portfolio"). But instead of mapping growth against share, you will put the importance of each SLU on the y-axis and the satisfaction it brings on the x-axis. Plot each SLU with a bubble, making the size of the bubble roughly proportional to the percentage of time in a week you spend on it.

In the top-left quadrant, you will find the SLUs of high importance and low satisfaction. These are areas of high urgency, because you care about these activities deeply but aren't focusing on them enough to get the most out of them. The SLUs in the top-right quadrant also deserve some attention: You want to keep devoting significant time and energy to your most important and highest-satisfaction activities, and invest less in those that are less important (bottom left and right).

Finally, look at your entire 2×2 and ask yourself: Does my current portfolio of SLUs put me on the right track to support my purpose and achieve my vision? Does it bring me closer to how I define a great life? Where can I save and reallocate my time? Just as in corporate strategy projects, you want to set some high-level priorities—rather than a detailed plan—for investments of your time, energy, and money.

When Toni, an engineer, completed this exercise, he saw four areas for urgent improvement in the top-left quadrant: significant other (since he didn't have one), mental health/mindfulness, societal engagement, and education/learning. His job/career SLU was split between two quadrants, and he was spending too much time on online entertainment, which charted in the bottom-right quadrant. It became clear to Toni what he needed to change.

5. What can I learn from benchmarks?

In almost every strategy project, we do a best practice and benchmarking analysis to understand what we can learn from leading companies. We can do the same for individuals by looking at role models and then, more importantly, at the research on life satisfaction (see the exhibit "Benchmarking life satisfaction").

Ask yourself: Who conducts their personal and professional life in a way I admire? Maybe it is a coworker caring for his bedridden parent, the mother of three at your kids' school who also manages payroll for a *Fortune* 500 company, or your religious leader who lives his purpose. Ask yourself what makes them admirable and what choices they would make if they were in your shoes.

A sample strategic life portfolio

This 2 × 2 shows that the subject needs to spend more time and energy on his significant other, mental health/mindfulness, societal engagement, and education/learning SLUs. He should spend less time on online entertainment—an area of low importance.

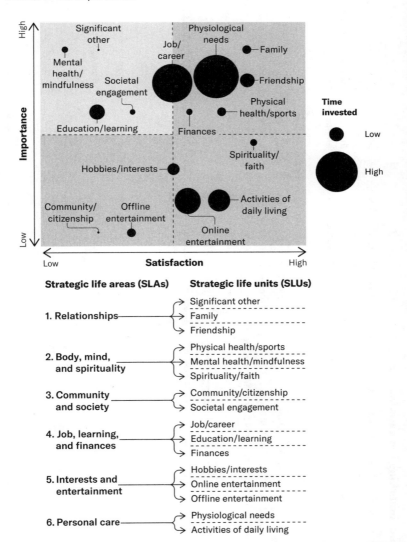

Benchmarking life satisfaction

One way to explore best practices is to understand where other people spend their time, energy, and money—and whether they report being satisfied with their lives. Longitudinal data from the German Socio-Economic Panel (SOEP) survey of almost 100,000 people from 1984 to 2019 is one source to reference. This chart shows one person's life satisfaction over time, with their satisfaction score reflecting changes to their baseline. Note that correlation does not equal causation.

Life satisfaction score as compared to baseline score (B), by strategic life area(s)

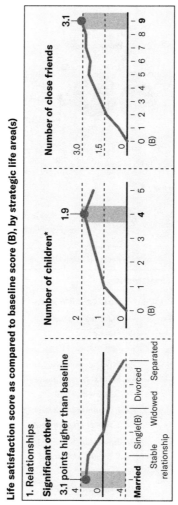

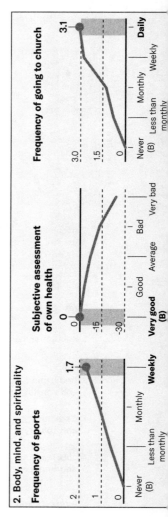

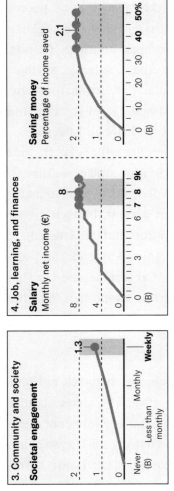
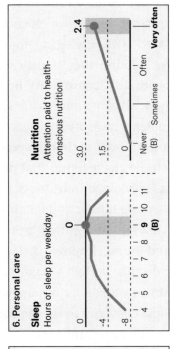

3. Community and society

Societal engagement

2

1

0

Never   Less than   Monthly   **Weekly**
(B)   monthly

1.3

4. Job, learning, and finances

Salary
Monthly net income (€)

8

4

0
(B)

0   3   6   **7**   **8**   **9k**

8

Saving money
Percentage of income saved

2

1

0
(B)

0   10   20   30   **40**   **50%**

2.1

5. Interests and entertainment

Leisure
Hours of spare time per
weekday

1

0

-1
(B)

0   1   2   **3**   **4**   5   6   7   8   9   10

1

6. Personal care

Sleep
Hours of sleep per weekday

0

-4

-8

4   5   6   7   8   **9**   10   11
                        (B)

0

Nutrition
Attention paid to health-
conscious nutrition

3.0

1.5

0

Never   Sometimes   Often   **Very often**
(B)

2.4

*If household income per person won't change.
Life satisfaction on a scale 0–100.

Now consider what scientific studies tell us about life satisfaction—not anecdotally but across large populations. We already mentioned the Harvard and Asia studies. One of the largest studies worldwide on life satisfaction is the German Socio-Economic Panel survey, which covered almost 100,000 people from 1984 to 2019, gathering more than 700,000 completed responses. It found that significant others, children, friends, sports, spirituality, community involvement, salaries, savings, and nutrition all contribute to life satisfaction. Not surprisingly, health problems have a very negative impact, and you can find an optimum amount of time to spend on leisure and sleep.

Other studies have found that proven life enhancers include practicing kindness, mindfulness, meditation, and gratefulness; cultivating more humor and laughter; dedicating time to learning; and developing a growth mindset (that is, believing your abilities and life can improve through effort and persistence).

As you do this work, it's important to understand and learn from what has worked for others, while also remembering that you can't just copy and paste someone else's approach. Your life strategy should be unique to you.

6. What portfolio choices can I make?

Corporate strategy is about making choices between options: Should we keep our current portfolio, diversify, focus, acquire a company, or enter a new market? In life, the equivalent questions are: What happens if I continue to live my life the way I am now? What if I change my priorities? Equipped with your definition of a great life, your purpose, your vision, your SLU ratings, and your benchmarks, you are ready to find out.

Go back to the great-life exercise in step 1 and think about what you can do for your areas of dissatisfaction. Review your purpose and vision from steps 2 and 3 and brainstorm how you might realize them. Think about the SLUs that step 4's portfolio exercise identified as needing more attention and how you can improve satisfaction or reallocate time there. Then consider how the insights gleaned from step 5's benchmarks can help you with all of the above. From this long list of potential changes and actions—small and large—select several that will best move you toward a great life, and commit to them.

Now you need to be specific about what you want to change. Examples from our workshop attendees include reconnecting with three friends from school, visiting one's grandfather every week, engaging in a weekly micro-adventure with one's significant other, changing jobs, committing to a new sleep schedule, trying a meditation app, starting a gratitude journal, spending more time with one's kids, exercising every day, supporting refugees, starting a social business, practicing religion again, dedicating 15 minutes to learning every day, switching college majors, converting a van into a camper to travel, and moving abroad. The possibilities are endless.

On the other hand, you have only 168 hours each week, which means you must reduce, outsource, or bundle existing activities, or make them more efficient through productivity strategies and tools. For example, when you work out with your boyfriend or volunteer for a good cause with your friends, you are bundling sports and significant other or societal engagement and friendship. Life strategy is about setting priorities; it is not about filling every waking minute. Remember to reserve space in your calendar for downtime as well. Researchers at the University of Pennsylvania's Wharton School and UCLA's Anderson School of Management found that people are happiest when they have two to five hours of free time each day.

When Judi, a workshop attendee, finished making her list of actions, she commented, "If I change all this, I will be a different person in a few weeks." Your life strategy could involve big steps like starting a business, traveling the world (as one of us did), or setting up a non-governmental organization, or it could involve a small step like meeting for coffee every week with people you care about. Even a minor change can have a big impact in two key ways. First, if you do it over and over again, you take advantage of the compound growth rate. Second, you are a node in a network of people, so your change not only affects those close to you but also ripples outward. After all, sometimes big changes are triggered by small, seemingly insignificant actions—the famous butterfly effect. For example, research has shown that doing just 15 minutes of physical activity a day increases life expectancy by three years (despite amounting to only about half a year of time investment). Exercise also gives you a dopamine boost, improving your mood, which benefits those around you and makes you more productive at work, potentially leading to new outputs that greatly impact the lives of others.

If you know which strategic life unit needs work but don't know what changes to make, dig deeper and develop a substrategy for that unit—a job/career strategy, a family strategy, a mental health/mindfulness strategy, and so on—just as each business unit does with the overarching corporate strategy.

For example, to develop a job/career strategy, ask yourself the following questions: How does my current job support my purpose and vision? Does my current job give me a sense of achievement and engagement (two of the six great-life dimensions)? How does my current job align with the strengths I identified in the purpose step? Finally, look for benchmarking data, such as BCG's Decoding Global Ways of Working study, where we list the top 10 criteria of great jobs according to more than 200,000 respondents. Again, rate how your job measures up to these criteria. The answers to these questions will give you an idea of how to move forward in your career.

7. How can I ensure a successful, sustained life change?

Change is not easy. Need proof? More than 40% of Americans set New Year's resolutions each January, and reports indicate that more than 90% fail to follow through on them.

Many companies, such as Google, ensure successful implementation of the strategies they've outlined by using OKRs (objectives and key results). OKRs are focused, ambitious, output-oriented, flexible, measurable, and transparent.

We recommend doing the same for each of the changes you committed to in step 6. Define the broad objective and the date by which you want to achieve it. Then break down each of those objectives into a few key results or action items, again with deadlines. Consider adding them directly to your calendar. If you are unsure about implementing a big move in your life, experiment. For example, Toni identified mental health/mindfulness as a high priority, so he might set an objective of "Download an app and try meditation techniques for 10 to 15 minutes a day (finish by the end of November)." He could then break it down into two key actions: (1) Review meditation apps and get started (first week of November), and (2) try an app for three weeks, review the experience, and make it a daily habit (last three weeks of November).

There are many ways that companies hold themselves to OKRs. Here, we focus on three of them. *Anchoring* means sharing your plan, as Google does by making its OKRs public. Whom will you tell about your plan or ask to join you on your journey? Strategy projects always involve small teams, so consider not only seeking input from others but also inviting one or two people to work on their own life strategies and then workshop everyone's results as a group. *Consequences* means setting up incentives for achievement, such as bonuses for success or penalties for failure. How will you reward yourself when you've successfully changed an aspect of your life, and what will the consequences be if you don't? And *check-ins* means routinely stepping back, refining and adjusting your efforts, and celebrating your achievements, as agile project development teams do. When can you spend 15 minutes each week to review and update your life strategy?

Toni, for example, might tell a friend to hold him to his changes, promise to donate a significant amount of money to a charitable cause if he doesn't stick to them, and schedule a weekly check-in with himself every Sunday before his study session.

Your One-Page Life Strategy

Often, the seeming enormity of an important task—such as life strategy development—is what stops us from doing it. So, to make what seems impossible possible, we recommend putting your entire life strategy on a single sheet of paper. We borrowed this idea from one-page summaries we have used in past strategy projects, and we saw it with Craig Perrett, a leadership coach who helps very senior executives at BCG manage their time after a successful career. If you have finished the exercises in this article, you can easily fill out this worksheet. Scan this QR code to download a PDF.

To start, write down what defines a great life for you. Next, record your strengths, your values, what lights you up, and what the world needs, and then add your purpose statement that incorporates those ideas. Third, summarize your life vision. Fourth, refer to that 2×2 you sketched and note the SLUs that are high priorities for action or that you spend too much time on. Next, write down the changes you'd like to make and commit to. Finally, for each of those changes, list an objective and two or three key results with deadlines, and then note the anchors, the consequences, and the check-in plan to make the change stick.

This page is your first minimum viable life strategy. As with corporate strategy, it needs to be reviewed, adjusted, and updated on a regular basis. Proprietary data from BCG suggests that 50% of companies review their strategy once a year, and 20% more than once a year—what we call *always-on strategy development*. Likewise, in addition to your weekly 15-minute check-in, we recommend scheduling a longer one- to two-hour review session with yourself, or with the life strategy group you started with other people, every six to 12 months. Review all seven steps, consider setbacks or shifting circumstances, and adjust accordingly.

The chief human resources officer we mentioned earlier puts her one-pager on top of all the papers on her desk. She looks at it every day to reinforce her belief in what makes a great life and to ensure she executes on her strategy for achieving it. When she has an idea for refinement, she writes it down. You can try that, too. A couple we worked with who wanted to develop life strategies in tandem went so far as to document their life purposes and goals with photos and notes in a picture frame. They hung it on the wall of their home, a daily reminder of where they want to go both together and as individuals.

Life is full of adventure and trauma, love and sadness, joy and stress. It can be great or terrible. There will be ups and downs. But a lot of it depends on you and the choices you make. A life strategy will not only guide you but also build your resilience so that you're better able to recover from missteps.

Sophia, a doctor who suffered from a serious chronic illness, wrote to us after attending a workshop: "I realized I want to make more decisions, do really crazy things, enjoy small and big moments, celebrate successes, go to places I've never been, meet people I've never seen before, take breaks in between, follow my flow, and make myself my most important project in life!"

Now, go and do the same. Your life is your top strategic priority.

Adapted from hbr.org, December 5, 2023. Reprint H07XDL

Discussion Guide

Are you feeling inspired by what you've read in this collection? Do you want to share the ideas in the articles or explore the insights you've gleaned with others? This discussion guide offers an opportunity to dig a little deeper, with questions to prompt personal reflection and start conversations with your team.

You don't need to have read the book from beginning to end to use this guide. Choose the questions that apply best to the articles you have read or that you feel might spark the liveliest discussion.

Reflect on key takeaways from your reading to help you adopt the ideas and techniques you want to integrate into your work as a leader. What tools can you share with your team to help everyone be their best? Becoming the leader you want to be starts with a detailed plan—and a commitment to carrying it out.

1. Daniel Goleman writes in "The Focused Leader" that "attention is the basis of the most essential of leadership skills." Where you focus yours will influence how you make decisions, help people find common ground, and enable you to be your authentic self. Reflect on how you manage alternating between focusing your attention on yourself, on others, and on the wider world. Think about a situation that required you to understand the broader context or market trends, to focus your attention beyond your team and your organization. How did you gather and process the information you needed to make a decision or move forward?

2. Consider a goal you struggled to achieve or did not meet. Which of the strategies in "Nine Things Successful People Do Differently," by Heidi Grant, do you think could have helped you overcome the challenges you faced?

3. What is a work habit that has endured for you? Describe the small steps you took to build it and the impact it had on your work. Have you ever considered experimenting with "habit stacking" to integrate new habits into a successful existing routine?

4. What types of tracking have helped you monitor and improve your progress on goals or a big project? How might keeping a daily work diary in some form help you navigate and overcome obstacles on an important project?

5. Have you ever directly asked trusted colleagues to name your strengths? Did they confirm your own beliefs or surprise you? How might you make soliciting feedback about your capabilities a regular part of your own professional development?

6. Think of a time when you successfully solicited actionable feedback from your manager or peers. How did you frame your questions to ensure you were receiving detailed feedback you could put into practice? What techniques did you use to steer the conversation to garner specific examples and concrete insights?

7. Reflect on a situation when you were able to use one of your core strengths at work. How did leaning into your skills impact your performance? What complemen-

tary skills might you develop to amplify your primary strengths? Is there a project or task that might benefit from cross-training your professional skills?

8. In "The Art of Asking Smarter Questions," the authors identify five types of questions: investigative, speculative, productive, interpretive, and subjective. Reflect on a time when you asked a question that led to a breakthrough in a project. What types of questions did you ask, and how did they help uncover critical information or insights? How did the quality of questions you asked influence the outcome?

9. Consider your network. Of the six types of connections Rob Cross and Robert J. Thomas mention in "A Smarter Way to Network" (people who provide you information, ideas, or expertise; people with formal or informal power; people who give you developmental feedback; people who lend you personal support; people who increase your sense of purpose; and people who promote your work/life balance), is there a category where you have a surplus of people? Or an area where you have few connections? What changes might you make to increase or reduce connections to better support your current work—and future goals?

10. Reflect on a time when you felt overwhelmed by the demands of helping others at work. How did this experience affect your productivity and well-being? What strategies from "Beat Generosity Burnout," by Adam Grant and Reb Rebele, are you interested in experimenting with to protect your time and energy the next time you're feeling overloaded?

11. Is it a curse to be labeled as talented? As a high performer, how have you successfully balanced the expectations of others with your own professional needs and goals? How does working on this balance contribute to your professional growth and overall satisfaction? Is there a difference between using your talent and trying to prove it?

12. In "Sleep Well, Lead Better," Christopher Barnes shares research that leaders who discount the value of sleep can negatively impact not just the emotions of the people on their teams but also their behaviors. Can you think of instances where you've experienced sleep devaluation— where a leader has communicated to you that sleep is unimportant or less important than a deadline or project? Consider whether you may have unintentionally sent this message to your own team through your words or actions. How might you model and support a culture that recognizes that sleep is a critical factor in performance?

13. When do you feel as though you are leading "in the flow" most at work? Is there a mindset you adopt or a lens through which you view your work to remain focused and present? How might you experiment with tapping into the five energies—purpose, wisdom, growth, love, and self-realization—Hitendra Wadhwa cites in "Leading in the Flow of Work" to navigate challenges?

14. Reflect on an instance when your high standards led to a positive outcome at work. Next consider a situation when your high standards caused challenges at work. What was the impact of maintaining these standards on the project

and on your colleagues? How did your pursuit of your standards impact the team performance and morale?

15. Have you ever applied strategic thinking to a personal goal? What inspired you to apply a professional practice to a nonwork challenge? How did this approach help you focus and make progress?

16. What other sources on high performance have had a significant impact on your work? Were there voices or subtopics you missed in this collection? Were there voices or subtopics included that surprised you?

17. After reading and reflecting on this book and discussing it with people on your team, write down the ideas and techniques you want to try. Think about how you might experiment and implement those in both the short term and the long term. Draft a plan to move forward.

Notes

Chapter 7: Beat Generosity Burnout

1. Mark C. Bolino et al., "'Well, I'm Tired of Tryin!': Organizational Citizenship Behavior and Citizenship Fatigue," *Journal of Applied Psychology* 100, no. 1 (2015): 56–74, https://doi.org/10.1037/a0037583; Joel Koopman, Klodiana Lanaj, and Brent A. Scott, "Integrating the Bright and Dark Sides of OCB: A Daily Investigation of the Benefits and Costs of Helping Others," *Academy of Management Journal* 59 (2016): 414–435, https://doi.org/10.5465/amj.2014.0262; Mark C. Bolino and William H. Turnley, "The Personal Costs of Citizenship Behavior: The Relationship Between Individual Initiative and Role Overload, Job Stress, and Work-Family Conflict," *Journal of Applied Psychology* 90, no. 4 (2005): 740–748, https://doi.org/10.1037/0021-9010.90.4.740.

2. Suzanne J. Peterson, Benjamin M. Galvin, and Donald Lange, "CEO Servant Leadership: Exploring Executive Characteristics and Firm Performance," *Personnel Psychology* 65 (2012): 565–596, https://doi.org/10.1111/j.1744-6570.2012.01253.x.

3. Adam M. Grant and David M. Mayer, "Good Soldiers and Good Actors: Prosocial and Impression Management Motives as Interactive Predictors of Affiliative Citizenship Behaviors," *Journal of Applied Psychology* 94, no. 4 (2009): 900–912, https://doi.org/10.1037/a0013770.

4. TEDx Talks, "You Don't Owe Anyone an Interaction, Caroline McGraw, TEDxBirminghamSalon," YouTube, October 13, 2016, https://www.youtube.com/watch?v=lwL4hjhkid4.

5. Stella E. Anderson and Larry J. Williams, "Interpersonal, Job, and Individual Factors Related to Helping Processes at Work," *Journal of Applied Psychology* 81, no. 3 (1996): 282–296, https://doi.org/10.1037/0021-9010.81.3.282.

6. Klodiana Lanaj, "Yes, Being Helpful Is Tiring," hbr.org, September 6, 2016, https://hbr.org/2016/09/research-yes-being-helpful-is-tiring.

7. Carolyn Gregoire, "The Giving Habits of Americans May Surprise You," HuffPost, August 20, 2013, updated December 6, 2017, https://www.huffpost.com/entry/are-you-a-giver-huffpost_n_3785215.

8. Adam M. Grant, "Does Intrinsic Motivation Fuel the Prosocial Fire? Motivational Synergy in Predicting Persistence, Performance, and Productivity," *Journal of Applied Psychology* 93, no. 1 (2008): 48–58, https://doi

.org/10.1037/0021-9010.93.1.48; Adam M. Grant and James W. Berry, "The Necessity of Others Is the Mother of Invention: Intrinsic and Prosocial Motivations, Perspective Taking, and Creativity," *Academy of Management Journal* 54 (2011): 73–96, https://doi.org/10.5465/amj.2011.59215085; Netta Weinstein and Richard M. Ryan, "When Helping Helps: Autonomous Motivation for Prosocial Behavior and Its Influence on Well-Being for the Helper and Recipient," *Journal of Personality and Social Psychology* 98, no. 2 (2010): 222–244, https://doi.org/10.1037/a0016984.

    9. Sonja Lyubomirsky, Kennon M. Sheldon, and David Schkade, "Pursuing Happiness: The Architecture of Sustainable Change," *Review of General Psychology* 9, no. 2 (2005): 111–131, https://doi.org/10.1037/1089 -2680.9.2.111.

    10. Adam A. Rapp, Daniel G. Bachrach, and Tammy L. Rapp, "The Influence of Time Management Skill on the Curvilinear Relationship Between Organizational Citizenship Behavior and Task Performance," *Journal of Applied Psychology* 98, no. 4 (2013): 668–677, https://doi .org/10.1037/a0031733.

    11. Joyce K. Fletcher, "Relational Practice: A Feminist Reconstruction of Work," *Journal of Management Inquiry* 7, no. 2 (1998): 163–186, https://doi .org/10.1177/105649269872012.

    12. Deborah L. Kidder, "The Influence of Gender on the Performance of Organizational Citizenship Behaviors," *Journal of Management* 28, no. 5 (2002): 629–648, https://doi.org/10.1177/014920630202800504.

    13. Oliver S. Curry et al., "Happy to Help? A Systematic Review and Meta-Analysis of the Effects of Performing Acts of Kindness on the Well-Being of the Actor," OSF preprints, September 2016, doi:10.31219/osf.io/ytj5s; Roy F. Baumeister et al., "Some Key Differences Between a Happy Life and a Meaningful Life," *Journal of Positive Psychology* 8, no. 6 (2013): 505–516, doi:10.1080/17439760.2013.830764.

Chapter 8: The Talent Curse

    1. Michael A. Hogg, "Uncertainty–Identity Theory," in M. P. Zanna, ed., *Advances in Experimental Social Psychology*, vol. 39 (Cambridge, MA: Academic Press, 2007), 69–126.

    2. Elaine S. Elliott and Carol S. Dweck, "Goals: An Approach to Motivation and Achievement," *Journal of Personality and Social Psychology* 54, no. 1 (1988): 5–12, https://doi.org/10.1037/0022-3514.54.1.5.

    3. Herminia Ibarra, "The Authenticity Paradox," *Harvard Business Review*, January–February 2015, https://hbr.org/2015/01/the-authenticity-paradox.

    4. Alice Miller, *The Drama of the Gifted Child: The Search for the True Self* (New York: Basic Books, 2008).

Quick Read: Sleep Well, Lead Better

1. Earl S. Ford, Timothy J. Cunningham, and Janet B. Croft, "Trends in Self-Reported Sleep Duration Among US Adults from 1985 to 2012," *Sleep* 38, no. 5, (May 2015): 829–832, https://doi.org/10.5665/sleep.4684.

2. Cristiano L. Guarana and Christopher M. Barnes, "Lack of Sleep and the Development of Leader-Follower Relationships over Time," *Organizational Behavior and Human Decision Processes* 141 (2017): 57–73, https://doi.org/10.1016/j.obhdp.2017.04.003.

3. Christopher M. Barnes et al., "'You Wouldn't Like Me When I'm Sleepy': Leaders' Sleep, Daily Abusive Supervision, and Work Unit Engagement," *Academy of Management Journal* 58 (2015): 1419–1437, https://doi.org/10.5465/amj.2013.1063.

4. Christopher M. Barnes et al., "Too Tired to Inspire or Be Inspired: Sleep Deprivation and Charismatic Leadership," *Journal of Applied Psychology* 101, no. 8 (2016): 1191–1199, https://doi.org/10.1037/apl0000123.

5. Christopher M. Barnes, "Sleep-Deprived People Are More Likely to Cheat," hbr.org, May 31, 2013, https://hbr.org/2013/05/sleep-deprived-people-are-more-likely-to-cheat.

6. Klodiana Lanaj, Russell E. Johnson, and Christopher M. Barnes, "Beginning the Workday Yet Already Depleted? Consequences of Late-Night Smartphone Use and Sleep," *Organizational Behavior and Human Decision Processes* 124, no. 1 (2014): 11–23, https://doi.org/10.1016/j.obhdp.2014.01.001.

7. Christopher M. Barnes, Jared A. Miller, and Sophie Bostock, "Helping Employees Sleep Well: Effects of Cognitive Behavioral Therapy for Insomnia on Work Outcomes," *Journal of Applied Psychology* 102, no. 1 (2017): 104–113, https://doi.org/10.1037/apl0000154.

8. Olaf Lahl et al., "An Ultra Short Episode of Sleep Is Sufficient to Promote Declarative Memory Performance," *Journal of Sleep Research* 17, no. 1 (2008): 3–10, doi: 10.1111/j.1365-2869.2008.00622.x.

About the Contributors

Teresa M. Amabile is the Edsel Bryant Ford Professor, Emerita, at Harvard Business School. A psychologist who has researched creativity, motivation, and everyday work life, she is the coauthor of *The Progress Principle: Using Small Wins to Ignite Joy, Engagement, and Creativity at Work* and *Retiring: Creating a Life That Works for You*.

Allison Bailey is a senior partner and a managing director at BCG. She leads the firm's People & Organization practice globally and is a coauthor of several publications on the future of work, the bionic company, digital learning, and upskilling. She is also a fellow of the BCG Henderson Institute.

Christopher M. Barnes is a Michael G. Foster Professor of Organizational Behavior in the Michael G. Foster School of Business at the University of Washington. He worked in the Fatigue Countermeasures branch of the Air Force Research Laboratory before pursuing his PhD in organizational behavior at Michigan State University and his Master of Science in sleep medicine from the University of Oxford's Sleep and Circadian Neuroscience Institute.

Jean-Louis Barsoux is a term research professor at IMD and a coauthor of *ALIEN Thinking: The Unconventional Path to Breakthrough Ideas*.

Alison Beard is an executive editor at *Harvard Business Review* and cohost of the *HBR IdeaCast* podcast. She previously worked as a reporter and editor at the *Financial Times*.

Brianna Barker Caza is a professor of management in the Bryan School of Business and Economics at the University of North Carolina at Greensboro. She received her PhD in organizational psychology from the University of Michigan.

Arnaud Chevallier is a professor of strategy at IMD and a coauthor of *Solvable: A Simple Solution to Complex Problems*.

James Clear is an entrepreneur and the author of *Atomic Habits: An Easy and Proven Way to Build Good Habits and Break Bad Ones.*

Rob Cross is the Edward A. Madden Professor of Global Leadership at Babson College and a senior vice president of research at the Institute for Corporate Productivity. He is the coauthor of *The Microstress Effect: How Little Things Add Up—and What to Do About It* (Harvard Business Review Press, 2023) and the author of *Beyond Collaboration Overload* (Harvard Business Review Press, 2021).

Frédéric Dalsace is a professor of marketing and strategy at IMD (Lausanne). He is the coauthor of several HBR articles and coauthor (with Goutam Challagalla) of the forthcoming book *Clean Winners: Sustainability Strategy That Puts Customers First* (Harvard Business Review Press, 2026).

Jane E. Dutton is the Robert L. Kahn Distinguished University Professor of Business Administration and Psychology, Emerita, at the University of Michigan's Ross School of Business. She is a cofounder of the Center for Positive Organizations at Ross.

Susanne Dyrchs is the chief of staff at BCG U, BCG's global specialty business for capability building, enablement, and upskilling. She is a people strategist and the coauthor of numerous publications on organization strategy, learning, leadership, and talent management. She has written a personal account of her transformational journey, *Wir-Zeit [Us Time]*.

Scott K. Edinger is a consultant, adviser, speaker, and the author of *The Growth Leader*. He is the coauthor of *The Hidden Leader* and *The Inspiring Leader*. Scott creates positive change for clients and is recognized as an expert on the intersection of leadership, strategy, and sales.

Joseph Folkman is the president of Zenger Folkman, a leadership development consultancy. He is the author of *The Trifecta of Trust: The Proven Formula for Building and Restoring Trust*.

Daniel Goleman, best known for his writing on emotional intelligence, was the cofounding director of the Consortium for Research on Emotional Intelligence in Organizations (CREIO) at Rutgers University. With his fellow CREIO codirector, Cary Cherniss, he wrote his latest book, *Optimal*, which reviews decades of research on the individual and collective power of emotional intelligence. The Daniel Goleman Emotional

Intelligence program offers training online. His other books include *Primal Leadership: Unleashing the Power of Emotional Intelligence* and *Altered Traits: Science Reveals How Meditation Changes Your Mind, Brain, and Body.*

Adam Grant is the Saul P. Steinberg Professor of Management and an organizational psychologist at the Wharton School. He is the author of *Think Again* and the host of the podcast *WorkLife*.

Heidi Grant is a social psychologist who researches, writes, and speaks about the science of motivation. Her books include *Reinforcements: How to Get People to Help You, Nine Things Successful People Do Differently,* and *No One Understands You and What to Do About It* (Harvard Business Review Press, 2018, 2015, and 2012, respectively). She is the Director of Behavioral Science and Insights for EY Americas.

Emily Heaphy is a professor of management and John F. Kennedy faculty fellow at the Isenberg School of Management at the University of Massachusetts Amherst. Her research focuses on interpersonal relationships, emotions, and the human body at work.

Steven J. Kramer is a retired researcher, writer, and consultant in Amherst, Massachusetts. He is a coauthor of "Inner Work Life" and "The Power of Small Wins"(*Harvard Business Review*, August 2002 and May 2011, respectively), and the coauthor of *The Progress Principle: Using Small Wins to Ignite Joy, Engagement, and Creativity at Work* (Harvard Business Review Press, 2011).

Sabina Nawaz is an executive coach who advises C-level executives and teams at *Fortune* 500 corporations, government agencies, nonprofits, and academic institutions around the world. She has spoken at hundreds of seminars, events, and conferences, including TEDx, and has written for the *Wall Street Journal, Fast Company, Inc.*, and *Forbes* in addition to hbr.org. She is the author of *You're the Boss: Become the Manager You Want to Be (and Others Need)*.

Gianpiero Petriglieri is an associate professor of organizational behavior at INSEAD. He directs the INSEAD Management Acceleration Programme and runs leadership workshops and master classes for global organizations.

Jennifer Petriglieri is an associate professor of organizational behavior at INSEAD and the author of *Couples That Work: How Dual-Career Couples Can Thrive in Love and Work* (Harvard Business Review Press, 2019).

Robert E. Quinn is a professor emeritus at the University of Michigan's Ross School of Business and a cofounder of its Center for Positive Organizations.

Reb Rebele is a senior research fellow for Wharton People Analytics and teaches management at Melbourne Business School.

Deborah Grayson Riegel is a professional speaker and facilitator, as well as a communication and presentation skills coach. She teaches leadership communication at Duke University's Fuqua School of Business and has taught at the Wharton School, Columbia Business School's Women in Leadership Program, and Peking University's International MBA Program. She is the author of *Overcoming Overthinking: 36 Ways to Tame Anxiety* *for Work, School, and Life* and the bestselling *Go to Help: 31 Strategies to Offer, Ask for, and Accept Help.*

Laura Morgan Roberts is the Frank M. Sands Sr. Associate Professor of Business Administration at the University of Virginia's Darden School of Business. She is an organizational psychologist and the coeditor of *Race, Work, and Leadership: New Perspectives on the Black Experience* (Harvard Business Review Press, 2019).

Gretchen M. Spreitzer is the Keith E. and Valerie J. Alessi Professor of Business Administration and a professor of Management and Organizations at the University of Michigan's Ross School of Business. Her research focuses on employee empowerment and leadership development, particularly within the context of organizational change and decline.

Rainer Strack is a senior partner emeritus and a senior adviser at BCG, where he built up and led the global People Strategy topic for 10 years. In 2014 he gave a widely watched TED Talk on the global workforce crisis. He formerly coheaded the Future of Work initiative for the World Economic Forum, and in 2021 he was inducted into *Personalmagazin*'s HR Hall of Fame. He is a fellow of the BCG Henderson Institute.

Anne Sugar is an executive coach and keynote speaker who has advised senior leaders at top organizations including TripAdvisor, HubSpot, Sanofi Genzyme, and Havas. A coach for Harvard Business School Executive Education and a guest lecturer at MIT, Anne draws on her decades of real world management expertise, including her role as SVP of Media at Digitas, where she led a team of 75 and managed *Fortune* 500 clients such as General Motors and Delta.

Robert J. Thomas is a managing director of Accenture Strategy. He is the author of eight books on leadership and organizational change, including *Crucibles of Leadership*, and the coauthor of *Geeks and Geezers* and *Driving Results Through Social Networks*.

Hitendra Wadhwa is a professor at Columbia Business School and the founder and CEO of Mentora Institute, a New York–based firm focused on performance acceleration and leadership development. He has also recently founded Mentora School for a Higher Age, a nonprofit organization that is developing a new generation of transformative changemakers across education, business, health care, policymaking, social justice, and other sectors.

Karen Walker is an executive coach and consultant who advises CEOs and senior leaders on thriving in hypergrowth and a high performance consultant who partners with CEOs and senior leaders. She works with *Fortune* 500 and high-growth companies to drive business "up and to the right" through strategy, expansion, and reorganization. She helped lead the then-fastest growing company in American history, growing it from $0 to $15 billion in revenue.

John H. Zenger is the CEO of Zenger Folkman, a leadership development consultancy, and the author or coauthor of 15 books including *The New Extraordinary Leader* and *The Extraordinary Coach*.

Index

Work is hard. Let us help.

Engage with HBR content the way you want, on any device.

Whether you run an organization, a team, or you're trying to change the trajectory of your own career, let *Harvard Business Review* be your guide. Level up your leadership skills by subscribing to HBR.

HBR is more than just a magazine—it's access to a world of business insights through articles, videos, audio content, charts, ebooks, case studies, and more.